Behavior Modification in Child, School, and Family Mental Health

An Annotated Bibliography on Applications with Parents and Teachers and in Marriage and Family Counseling

Daniel G. Brown
U. S. Public Health Service
Phoenix Area Indian Health Service
Mental Health Branch, Phoenix, Arizona

RESEARCH PRESS COMPANY
2612 North Mattis Ave.
CHAMPAIGN, ILLINOIS 61820

CIP
Library of Congress Cataloging in Publication Data

Brown, Daniel G   1924-
     Behavior modification in child, school and family mental health.

     1. Behavior therapy—Abstracts. 2. Mentally handicapped
children—care and treatment—Abstracts.
I. Title.
RJ505.B4B75   016.6189′28′91   72-7372

ISBN 0-87822-074-7

Copies of this book may be ordered from the publisher at the
address given on the title page.

Foreword

Unlike conventional psychotherapy, behavior therapy—as used here, a term synonymous with behavior modification—has always concerned itself with inter- as well as intra-individual events. At first, the emphasis was primarily upon the modification of the individual's behavior as it impinged upon others. Gradually, as the complex contingencies of behavioral interchange became more fully appreciated, it came to be recognized that a total behavior modification program had also to involve the behavioral modification of significant others in the individual's life. Not withstanding the fact that some 90% of the behavior modification literature has emerged within the past decade, for the most part only the more recent publications reflect this trend—a situation which makes the task of the discriminating bibliographer rather difficult.

Not so long ago, the compilation of a behavior modification bibliography was relatively straightforward. One systematically included everything and left the reader, usually a research psychologist or avant-garde professional, to decide whether or not any particular reference met his particular needs. But nowadays the literature is vast and the basic terminology of behavior modification familiar to most mental health practitioners and many parents and teachers, so that reader and bibliographer alike can choose to be selective. But even the most selective of mere listings of resource material provides no exemption from the necessity for the reader to have both time and a first-class library readily available. And even then it is possible to learn only about items actually in print.

Many a bibliographer has essayed to cope with these difficulties but few have succeeded. Attempts range from the shiny and expensive hard cover library edition to the mimeoed handout. There are even bibliographies of bibliographies. Of all such compilations, that of Dr. Brown goes furthest towards meeting the exacting, at times, diverse requirements of the practitioner, teacher, parent, family and marriage counselor, and all who must have complete and up-to-date information about pertinent books, articles, films, and tapes at their finger tips. The balance between comprehension and selectivity is nicely preserved, and "annotation" is a concept which Dr. Brown takes most seriously. The outcome is a readable yet succinct assemblage of virtually everything the busy practitioner needs to know, including names, addresses, prices, and other "vital statistics." Hopefully, this timely new venture, inexpensive yet invaluable, will be reprinted in many new editions in the coming years and even be expanded to cover the individual in environments other than the home and school. All in all, both Dr. Brown and Research Press are to be congratulated.

Cyril M. Franks, Ph.D.
Professor of Psychology and Director,
The Psychological Clinic
The Graduate School, Rutgers University
       and
Editor, *Behavior Therapy*

Preface

The purpose of this bibliography is to provide workers in mental health, education, counseling, and related fields with an up-to-date guide to the rapidly growing literature concerned with the applicability of behavior modification principles and procedures with children in family, school, and special environments; a section on marriage and family counseling rounds out the range of applications of behavioral procedures within the home setting.

Sharply contrasted to the long-established clinical method which emphasizes intrapsychic pathology, psychodiagnostic evaluations, and individual psychotherapy is the behavioral approach to mental health. There is now convincing evidence that the behavioral analysis and modification model has a number of important advantages when compared to traditional therapy: it is more effective, economic, and specific in outcome; it is applicable to a wider range of disturbed and handicapped children; and it can be carried out not only by professionals but also by others concerned with children. This latter benefit means, for example, that parents, teachers, or aides in special settings can be trained in behavior modification procedures to function as primary change agents and principal "therapists" for disturbed children. It also means that married couples and family members can utilize behavioral techniques to reduce conflicts and disharmony and to increase positive, mutually supportive behaviors. The behavioral model is now becoming more widely recognized and more firmly established in mental health, education, and allied disciplines; professional workers in these fields will be increasingly called upon to provide consultation and training for non-professional helping agents in the community.

This volume is a revised and updated expansion of a bibliography published by the National Clearinghouse for Mental Health Information, National Institute of Mental Health in 1971.* The references in the first three sections have been substantially increased, and three sections have been added to this edition: (1) Applications in Special Settings for Children and Youth, (2) Applications in Marriage and Family Counseling, and (3) Films. Attesting to the growth of behavioral literature, about 90% of the 241 references in this selection have been published or presented in the last six years and approximately two-thirds within the last three years.

The address of the author of each paper and the publisher, address, and price of books and films have been included to help the reader secure particular references without having to consult other sources.

Daniel G. Brown
Phoenix Indian High School
Phoenix, Arizona
August, 1972

*Publication No. (HSM) 71-9043, 1971, U. S. Department of Health, Education and Welfare, Public Health Service, Health Services and Mental Health Administration, 5600 Fishers Lane, Rockville, Maryland 20852.

vi

Sound strategy would concentrate our innovative efforts upon the young, in programs for children and youth, for parents, and for teachers and others who work directly with children. . . . We feel that fully half of our mental health resources—money, facilities, people— should be invested in programs for children and youth, for parents of young children, and for teachers and others who work directly with children. . . . New and more effective ways must be found to reach and help children where they are—in families and schools—and to assist these critically important social systems in fostering the good development of children and in coming to the child's support when the developmental course goes astray.**

**M. Brewster Smith and Nicholas Hobbs, "The community and the community mental health center," *American Psychologist*, 1966, *21*, 505.

Contents

Applications with Parents

1

Behavior Modification in Child, School, and Family Mental Health

---

1. Allen, K. E. and Harris, F. R. Elimination of a child's excessive scratching by training the mother in reinforcement procedures. *Behaviour Research and Therapy*, 1966, *4*, 79-84. Available from Dr. K. Eileen Allen, 143 Experimental Education Unit, Child Development & Retardation Center, WJ-110, University of Washington, Seattle, Washington 98105.

Reports on the case of a five-year-old girl whose face, neck, and other parts of her body were covered with open sores and scabs from repetitive scratching of about one year's duration. Mental health consultation in behavior modification was given to the mother who was trained to withhold all reinforcement including parental attention, concern, etc., in relation to the daughter's scratching but to give her liberal reinforcements (e.g., praise, attention, gold stars with back-up reinforcements: goodies, refreshments, items for her Barbie doll, etc.) for desirable behaviors including periods of not scratching. Within six weeks and after seven consultation-training sessions with the mother, the girl's scratching behavior had been eliminated and her face and body were clear of sores and scabs; a follow-up four months later showed no further recurrence.

2. Barrett, B. H. Behavior modification in the home: Parents adopt laboratory-developed tactics to bowel-train a 5½-year old. *Psychotherapy, Theory, Research and Practice*, 1969, *6*, 172-176. Available from Dr. Beatrice H. Barrett, Behavior Prosthesis Laboratory, Box C, Waverley, Massachusetts 02178.

Report of a bowel-trained five-and-one-half-year-old boy whose parents, with only limited mental health consultative assistance in the use of behavior modification procedures, were able to help their son establish complete bowel control. The author noted that this accomplishment, which was made in less than two and one half months, illustrates how parents, with professional assistance, may be

1

helped to cope with seemingly unmanageable children in their own homes.

3. Becker, W. C. *Parents are teachers: A child management program.* 1971, 194 pp., $3.75 paper; *A group leader's guide for parents are teachers,* 1971. 48 pp., $2.00 paper. Research Press, Box 3177 Country Fair Station, Champaign, Illinois 61820.

A manual written specifically to help parents understand and learn how to use behavior modification procedures with their own children. Operant reinforcement is a central concept throughout: kinds of reinforcers, when and how to reinforce, using stronger reinforcers, reinforcement and punishment, etc. Includes many examples and illustrations and provides exercises for parents to carry out in learning how to cope effectively with their children. This manual and accompanying guide would be helpful in consultative work and training programs with parents.

4. Bernal, M. E. Training parents in child management. In Robert H. Bradfield (Ed.), *Behavioral modification of learning disabilities.* Academic Therapy Publications, 1539 Fourth St., San Rafael, California 94901, 1971. $3.95 paper.

A thorough, clearly written account of how the author, a mental health professional, carries out her parent training program involving children with various deviant behaviors and emotional disturbances. This innovative and significant parent training program includes: contemporary behavioral analysis of family interactions, home observations, baseline and other record-keeping practices, use of closed circuit television both for live recordings of family interactions as well as for training parents in the use of reinforcement contingencies, etc. The case of a preschool-age, hyperactive, unmanageable boy is described in detail to illustrate the step-by-step procedures and applications of behavior modification carried out by the parents under the guidance of the author. This applied research-demonstration work is particularly relevant to treatment and preventive services for children in community mental health centers and outpatient clinics. For other related, important contributions of Bernal, see Behavior modification and the brat syndrome, *Journal of Consulting and Clinical Psychology*, 1968, *32*, 447-455; Behavioral feedback in the modification of brat behaviors, *Journal of Nervous and Mental Diseases*, 1969, *148*, 375-385; and The use of videotape feedback and operant learning principles in training parents in management of deviant children. Paper presented at the Annual Meeting of the Association for Advancement of Behavior Therapy, Miami Beach, Florida, 1970. These materials are available from Dr. Martha E. Bernal, Psychology Department, University of Denver, Denver, Colorado 80210.

5. Boardman, W. K. Rusty: A brief behavior disorder. *Journal of Consulting Psychology*, 1962, *26*, 293-297. Available from Dr. William K. Boardman, Department of Psychology, University of Georgia, Athens, Georgia 30601.

Case of a six-year-old boy, Rusty, with multiple deviant behaviors: enuresis, stealing, frequent defiance, rebelliousness, aggressiveness, running away from school, manipulation of others, etc. The mental health professional, who saw Rusty one time and then only for a few minutes, worked with the mother in terms of training her to utilize basic reinforcement procedures with her son. In less than one week Rusty's serious behavior problems had been largely eliminated and had remained so approximately a year later. This case represents one of the earlier ones reported in the literature in which the parent, with mental health consultation, functioned as the primary change agent or "therapist" for her own child. Note: For theoretical interpretations of the case of Rusty in terms of a behavior modification model versus a psychodynamic model, see respectively, Bandura, A., Punishment revisited, and Miller, D. R., On the definition of problems and the interpretation of symptoms; both in *Journal of Consulting Psychology*, 1962, *26*, 298-301 (Bandura) and 302-305 (Miller).

6. Browning, R. M. Experimental-clinical treatment of severely emotionally disturbed children. Unpublished paper, 1971. Available from Dr. Robert M. Browning, Wisconsin Children's Treatment Center, 3418 Harper Rd., Madison, Wisconsin 53704.

Describes an intensive children's residential behavior modification treatment project initiated in the spring of 1971 involving six severely emotionally disturbed children, five to nine years of age. A unique and major component of this research project, which is designed to limit residential treatment to a period of approximately six months, is concerned with training parents to carry out behavior modification procedures when their child returns home. For this purpose, the author has developed a Parents' Training Manual in Behavior Modification.

7. Clement, P. W. Please, Mother, I'd rather you do it yourself: Training parents to treat their own children. *Journal of School Health*, 1971, *61*, 65-69. Available from Dr. Paul W. Clement, Fuller Graduate School of Psychology, 177 North Madison, Pasadena, California 91101.

Outlines and discusses the steps involved in the training of parents by mental health professionals in the use of behavior modification principles and procedures for coping with various behavior problems of their own children including specifying and recording target behaviors, deciding on priorities for what behaviors to be changed first, modeling the behavioral procedures to be carried out by the parent,

3

providing consultative training with the family in the home, etc. The case of an eight-year-old boy, whose major problem was sleepwalking, is used to illustrate the parent training process. In addition, the author reports on the training of small groups of parents of preschoolers, along with the use of peers, to treat the problems of their own children.

8. Coe, W. C. A family operant program. Paper presented to the Annual Meeting of the Western Psychological Association, Los Angeles, California, 1970. Available from Dr. William C. Coe, Department of Psychology, Fresno State College, Fresno, California 93726.

A brief report and discussion on the use of behavior modification in working with parents of children or adolescents with various behavior problems and interpersonal difficulties in the home and school (tantrums, truancy, low achievement, negativism, non-compliance, etc.). In each case, the parents and the child were asked to formulate three lists of behaviors: (1) the "Do's," i.e., behaviors that both parents and child agree he should do but has difficulty doing; (2) the "Don'ts," i.e., behaviors that both parents and child agree he does but should not do; and (3) the "Reinforcers," i.e., activities or things that the child likes most. A point and monetary system is used in relation to these lists in which the child receives payment for behaviors in the "Do's" but must pay for those in the "Don'ts" and "Reinforcers" categories. The case of a twelve-year-old boy and his parents is described to demonstrate how this approach was carried out.

9. Engeln, R., Knutson, J., Laughy, L., and Garlington, W. Behavior modification techniques applied to a family unit—A case study. *Journal of Child Psychology and Psychiatry*, 1968, *9*, 245-252. Available from Dr. Warren Garlington, Department of Psychology, Washington State University, Pullman, Washington 99163.

Reports on the use of operant reinforcement with a family of a six-year-old boy whose extremely aggressive, destructive, and unmanageable behaviors made life almost impossible for his family and anyone else who came into contact with him. Work was carried out with the boy's mother, father, and an older brother on a weekly outpatient basis. The mother observed and was trained by mental health professionals in systematic reinforcement procedures with her son, both in the clinic and at home. Substantial progress was made in bringing about significant increases in socially appropriate and cooperative behavior.

10. Galloway, C. and Galloway, K. C. *Parent groups with a focus on precise behavior management,* VII, No. I. Institute on Mental Retardation and Intellectual Development, John F. Kennedy Center for Research on Education and Human Development, Peabody College for

Teachers, Nashville, Tennessee 37203, 1970. 38 pp. Single copies available on request.

Report of a group parent training project at a day care center for mentally retarded children. Parents were trained to carry out behavior modification procedures at home with their own retarded children, utilizing the four-step system of Lindsley of: (1) pinpointing, (2) recording, (3) consequating, and (4) trying again. Illustrations of the parent training project are discussed in terms of work with the parents of four children with behaviors selected for modification.

11. Gardner, J. E., Pearson, D. T., Bercovici, A. N., and Bricker, D. E. Measurement, evaluation, and modification of selected social interactions between a schizophrenic child, his parents, and his therapist. *Journal of Consulting and Clinical Psychology*, 1968, *32*, 543-549. Available from Dr. James E. Gardner, 1100 Glendon, Suite 1425, Los Angeles, California 90024.

Report on the development of an operant reinforcement outpatient training-treatment program of a six-year-old, middle class boy and his parents. This boy showed multiple deviant and psychotic behaviors over a two-year period and had been twice diagnosed as schizophrenic. After 15 consultative sessions, which included training the parents in the use of behavior modification procedures with their son, this boy's behaviors were characterized as essentially normal and appropriate and he was able to be enrolled in a regular school class. See also the senior author's paper on counseling parents in the use of behavior modification procedures in the home that brought about the elimination of seizure behavior in their ten-year-old daughter: Behavior therapy treatment approach to a psychogenic seizure case. *Journal of Consulting Psychology*, 1967, *31*, 209-212.

12. Hall, R. V., Axelrod, S., Tyler, L., Grief, E., Jones, F. C., and Robertson, R. Modification of behavior problems in the home with a parent as observer and experimenter. *Journal of Applied Behavior Analysis*, 1972, *5*, 53-64. Available from Dr. R. Vance Hall, Bureau of Child Research, Juniper Gardens Children's Project, 2021 North Third, Kansas City, Kansas 66101.

Reports on four cases in which parents carried out behavior modification procedures with their own children. The behavior problems included: (1) use of an orthodontic device, (2) low-level performance of household tasks, (3) whining and shouting, and (4) long duration of dressing time. These behaviors were successfully modified by the parents who demonstrated that they were capable of making effective applications of operant principles in the home with their own children.

13. Hanf, C. Modifying problem behaviors in mother-child interaction: Standardized laboratory situations. Unpublished paper, 1970. Available from Dr. Constance Hanf, Child Development and Rehabilitation Center, University of Oregon Medical School, Portland, Oregon 97201.

The author reports on the use of standardized laboratory analogs of problem-producing parent-child interaction in the home as a means of training mothers to use behavior modification procedures in decelerating maladaptive and increasing desirable behaviors in their children. The training sessions, which involved not only modifying a single behavior but a broad range of behaviors, occurred twice weekly over a two to three month period with a maximum of 24 sessions and an average of 15 sessions for each mother-child pair. Eighteen mother-child pairs contributed to the development of the outpatient analog situation; all of the children, ages two to eight, were severely hyperactive and unmanageable and had one or more chronic, handicapping physical disability: cerebral palsy, deafness, speech problems, mental retardation, etc. The results suggest considerable promise for this approach to parent involvement in directly modifying the behavior of disturbed children. See also Hanf, C. Parent treatment-training program for disturbed mother-child behaviors. Paper prepared for presentation at the Nashville Showcase of Innovative Treatment Programs in Child Mental Health, Nashville, Tennessee, 1972.

14. Hawkins, R. P., Peterson, R. F., Schweid, E., and Bijou, S. W. Behavior therapy in the home: Amelioration of problem parent-child relations with the parent in a therapeutic role. *Journal of Experimental Child Psychology*, 1966, *4*, 99-107. Available from Dr. Robert P. Hawkins, Department of Psychology, Western Michigan University, Kalamazoo, Michigan 49001. Also in B. G. Guerney, Jr. (Ed.), *Psychotherapeutic agents: New roles for non-professionals, parents, and teachers.* Holt, Rinehart and Winston, 383 Madison Ave., New York, New York 10017, 1969. Pp. 401-407 $10.50.

Case of a four-year-old boy whose multiple undesirable behaviors were effectively modified in the home by the parent with guidance from mental health professionals. One of the early demonstrations of in-the-home applications of behavior modification. See also the senior author's paper, Universal parenthood training: A proposal for preventive mental health, 1971, mimeographed.

15. Herbert, E. W. Parent programs—Bringing it all back home. Paper presented at the Annual Meeting of the American Psychological Association, Miami Beach, Florida, 1970. Available from Dr. Emily W. Herbert, Kansas Center for Research in Mental Retardation and Human Development, University of Kansas, Lawrence, Kansas 66044.

Report on two mothers whose children were considered unacceptable for regular public school and were, therefore, enrolled in a special classroom. These mothers, who had previously carried out simple behavior modification procedures in the home using material reinforcements, were subsequently trained to observe and record (using a wrist counter) their attention to appropriate or desired behaviors in their children on a daily basis. This simple, economical technique was effective in producing desired changes in both parent and child.

16. Holland, C. J. An interview guide for behavioural counseling with parents. *Behavior Therapy*, 1970, *1*, 70-79. Available from Dr. Cornelius J. Holland, Department of Psychology, University of Windsor, Windsor, Ontario, Canada.

The author presents a 21-step outline developed for use in helping parents learn how to carry out behavior analysis and behavior modification in coping with problems with their own children Would be helpful as a training aid for mental health personnel in working with the parents of emotionally disturbed and other handicapped children.

17. Holzschuh, R. D. Little brother behavior improvement project, 1970. Unpublished material available from Dr. Ronald D. Holzschuh, Executive Director, Big Brothers of Greater Kansas City, 417 East 13th St., Kansas City, Missouri 64106. Price list available.

This material is used in connection with a behavior modification self-improvement project involving the Big Brother (BB)-Little Brother (LB) Program in Kansas City. Specific items include: (1) Program guidelines for LB behavior improvement project which involves the basic steps in behavior modification outlined by Lindsley of: (a) pinpointing behaviors to be modified, (b) recording and charting the frequency of occurrence, (c) changing conditions of the consequences, and (d) trying again if first effort to modify is not successful; (2) An Activity Card that records each time BB and LB are together, what happened, accomplishments of LB, etc.; (3) Daily behavioral progress record for each LB that lists specific behaviors to be increased (e.g., taking a bath or shower daily, making own bed, reading given number of pages, etc.) or to be decreased (biting fingernails, hitting others, errors in spelling, etc.); (4) A LB rating system and daily rate (or point) chart of cumulative improvements with special back-up reinforcements such as desired items from a Sears catalog, tickets to professional football, soccer, or major league baseball games, etc.; (5) List of specific behaviors in major categories such as personal care, social behaviors, home activities, money management, school skills, etc., that LB's select for modification and improvement.

18. Howard, O. F. Teaching a class of parents as reinforcement therapists to treat their own children. Paper presented at the Annual Meeting of the Southeastern Psychological Association, Louisville, Kentucky, 1970. 15 pp. mimeographed, $2.00. Available from Dr. Oscar F.

Howard, Lookout Region Shared Services, Box 29, Lafayette, Georgia 30728.

A group of ten parents met with mental health professionals for six sessions for the purpose of learning how to carry out behavior modification procedures with their own emotionally disturbed children. The parents were heterogenous in racial, socioeconomic, and educational composition. The training sessions used a variety of techniques including reading assignments, films, role playing, open discussions, how to use a point-system reinforcement contingency approach, etc. Results were quite favorable in demonstrating the feasibility and effectiveness of group training and consultative work with parents as primary change agents for their own children. These results were in contrast to a control group of ten parents who showed no positive changes.

19. Johnson, C. A. The utilization of parents as change agents. Unpublished paper, 1971, 32 pp., mimeographed. Available from Dr. Claudia A. Johnson, Department of Psychology and Early Childhood Education Center, University of Utah, Salt Lake City, Utah 84112.
This paper presents a review and discussion of some 38 case studies and research reports concerned with the use of parents as the primary agents of change in bringing about the deceleration of deviant and acceleration of productive behaviors in their own children. Parents were trained both in the home and in the clinic-laboratory to carry out behavior modification procedures in coping with a wide variety of target behaviors in their children. The author has made a valuable contribution to the literature in outlining and summarizing all of these papers and in indicating the kinds of variables and considerations that need to be taken into account to increase the validity and reliability of work in this area. She concludes from these papers that parents indeed can be used as effective change agents.

20. Johnson, J. M. Using parents as contingency managers. *Psychological Reports*, 1971, *28*, 703-710. Available from Dr. James M. Johnson, Department of Psychology, State University College of Arts and Science, Plattsburgh, New York 12901.
Reports on the alleviation of disturbing behaviors of 18-months duration of two children, ages nine and eleven, during the dinner meal; techniques of extinction, avoidance, and fading were successfully carried out entirely by the parents within a period of 20 days. Problems encountered while instructing the parents in behavioral techniques are discussed.

21. Johnson, S. M. and Brown, R. A. Producing behavior change in parents of disturbed children. *Journal of Child Psychology and Psy-*

chiatry, 1969, *10*, 107-121. Available from Dr. Stephen M. Johnson, Psychology Clinic, 1679 Agate St., University of Oregon, Eugene, Oregon 97403.

Reports on outpatient behavior modification work with two parent-child cases: one involving a preschool-age girl, her mother, and grandmother; and the other, a six-year-old boy and his mother. Both children had multiple behavioral deviations: developmental retardation, hyperactivity, unmanageable conduct, inability to relate to peers, negativistic, destructive acts, etc. The therapist trained the parents in operant reinforcement procedures with their children, particularly by modeling the effective use of such procedures and then guiding the parents in carrying them out. In both cases, the parents were successful in bringing about substantial improvements in the behaviors of their own children.

22. Kuhlman, C. E. A training program for parents in child behavior management: Conceptualization, design, and evaluation. Prepublication paper, 1970. Available from Dr. Carl E. Kuhlman, Evans Learning Center, 1000 Speer Blvd., Denver, Colorado 80203.

The first half of this paper involves a brief review of the literature relative to programs concerned with training parents in behavior modification along with the implications of this development for child mental health, particularly in terms of community services and manpower utilization. The other half is devoted to a description of the Evans Learning Center, whose overall function is the rehabilitation of educationally deficient children, and with the Parent Training Program in Behavior Modification within the center, particularly the procedures used and suggested changes for the improvement of the latter. The author concludes with a proposed evaluation study of the effectiveness of the Parent Training Program as carried out at the Evans Center.

23. Lindsley, O. R. An experiment with parents handling behavior at home. *Johnstone Bulletin*, 1966, *9*, 27-36. Available from Dr. Ogden R. Lindsley, Bureau of Child Research, University of Kansas, 9 Bailey Hall, Lawrence, Kansas 66044.

Reports on the author's work with a group of fathers in the effective use of behavior modification with their retarded children in the home. Discusses the procedures used including the "Sunday Box" and the "Point Store." See also the author's paper, Operant behavior management: Background and procedures, which discusses Pavlovian and operant conditioning and outlines the basic steps in behavior modification of Pinpointing, Recording, Consequating, and Trying Again.

24. Madsen, C. K. and Madsen, C. H., Jr. *Parents/children/discipline: A positive approach*. Allyn and Bacon, Inc., 470 Atlantic Ave., Boston, Massachusetts 02210, 1972. 213 pp. $3.95 paper.

Written as a guide and resource book for parents in learning how to apply behavior modification procedures in decreasing problem behaviors and facilitating desirable, productive behaviors in their children. The contents are divided into three main sections. The first part of the book deals with the understanding of the principles that govern how children learn particular behaviors and with the step-by-step procedures necessary to modify these behaviors. The second part consists of 111 actual examples of children and youth with a very large variety of problem behaviors that were modified through the use of behavioral procedures; each example is outlined in terms of the specific behavior to be modified, the record of its frequency, the reinforcement contingencies arranged to change the behavior, and an evaluation of the effectiveness of the effort. The third part provides various lists of kinds and examples of positive and negative reinforcements (words, physical expression, activities, material things, etc.) that are used in parent-child relationships. This book would be helpful in training courses and consultation work with parents.

25. McIntire, R. W. *For love of children: Behavioral psychology for parents*. C. R. M. Books, Inc., Del Mar, California 92014, 1970. 208 pp. $6.95.

A book based on principles and applications of behavior modification and written specifically for parents of young, intermediate, and adolescent children. The first half of the book, "Parenthood by Design," is concerned primarily with behavioral guidelines governing normal childhood development, particularly the role of consequences, rewards, and punishments in parent-child behaviors. The second half, "Blueprints for Change," deals mainly with applications of behavior modification to a variety of problem behaviors including crying, tantrums, fears, compulsions, etc., along with those connected with self-care, toilet training, sleep, meals, money, sex, school, sociability, etc. A separate chapter is devoted to behavioral problems of teenagers. The concluding chapter summarizes the role of reinforcement in successful family living. This book, in whole or in part, could be used in consultative and training work with parents and as supplementary reading in college courses in child psychology and related subjects.

26. O'Leary, D. K., O'Leary, S., and Becker, W. C. Modification of a deviant sibling interaction pattern in the home. *Behaviour Research and Therapy*, 1967, *5*, 113-120. Available from Dr. K. Daniel O'Leary,

Department of Psychology, State University of New York, Stony Brook, New York 11790. Also in B. G. Guerney, Jr. (Ed.), *Psychotherapeutic agents: New roles for non-professionals, parents and teachers*. Holt, Rinehart and Winston, 383 Madison Ave., New York, New York 10017, 1969. Pp. 408-418 $10.50.

Reports on the effective use of a token reinforcement and time-out from reinforcement procedure with a six-year-old boy and his three-year-old brother who frequently engaged in a variety of deviant behaviors, including kicking, hitting, throwing things at each other, and other destructive acts. The treatment program was carried out in the home for several months and involved the parent (mother) learning to function as a therapist for these two brothers.

27. Ora, J. P. and Wagner, L. I. Contextual variables in oppositional child training. Paper presented at the Annual Meeting of the Southeastern Psychological Association, Louisville, Kentucky, 1970. Available from Dr. John P. Ora, Child and Youth Development Center, 3420 Richards St., Nashville, Tennessee 37215.

This paper describes a Regional Intervention Project for preschoolers and parents concerned with what Wahler has referred to as oppositional children and Bernal has called the Brat Syndrome, i.e., children with unmanageable, destructive, aversive, out-of-control behaviors. The project involves training the parents of oppositional, disturbed, and other handicapped children up to three or four years of age, in the use of behavior modification procedures. The parent and child interact in 20-minute structured play sessions, observed by behavioral consultants for the purpose of training the parent to carry out the procedures in the home. Following this training and the successful management of their own children, these parents in turn become behavioral managers themselves and carry out the training of other parents. See the senior author's, Instruction Pamphlet for Parents of Oppositional Children, developed for use in this project. For more recent developments of this project, see the senior author's paper, Regional intervention project for parents training other parents as therapists of preschool children with mental, emotional, and other handicaps. Paper prepared for presentation at the Nashville Showcase of Innovative Treatment Approaches to Child Mental Health, Nashville, Tennessee, 1972.

28. Patterson, G. R., Cobb, J. A., and Ray, R. S. A social engineering technology for retraining aggressive boys. Prepublication paper presented at the University of Georgia Symposium in Experimental-Clinical Psychology, Athens, 1970. Available from Dr. Gerald R. Patterson, Oregon Research Institute, 488 East 11th Ave., Eugene, Oregon 97403.

Detailed description and discussion of the implications of a parent training project conducted for eleven families with one or more unusually destructive, hyperaggressive boys, ages six to thirteen. Following ten hours of baseline behavioral observation in the home, small group meetings of three or four sets of these parents met one evening a week, usually for 5 to 8 weeks, for mental health training and consultation in the use of behavior modification procedures in decreasing the aggressive and increasing the positive behaviors in their sons. For a related discussion and case example of the significance of mental health personnel working with the parents of a child with disordered behaviors, rather than focusing directly on the disturbed child himself, see Patterson, G. R., McNeal, S., Hawkins, N., and Phelps, R. Reprogramming the social environment. *Journal of Child Psychology and Psychiatry*, 1967, *8*, 181-195.

29. Peine, H. A. Programming the home. Paper presented at the Annual Meeting of the Rocky Mountain Psychological Association, Albuquerque, New Mexico, 1969. Available from Dr. Hermann A. Peine, Bureau of Educational Research, University of Utah, Salt Lake City, Utah 84112.

Discusses the modification of screaming, biting self and others, and throwing of objects by a three-year-old prepsychotic boy. This was accomplished by the therapist working with the parents during a total of six visits to the home that averaged one hour each. Sixth month follow-up showed that the deviant behaviors rarely occurred. See also the author's paper, Home programming and parent training in the use of behavior modification procedures—A tutorial lecture, presented at the Annual Meeting of the Western Psychological Association, Los Angeles, California, 1970.

30. Peterson, R. F. Expanding the behavior laboratory: From clinic to home. Paper presented at the Annual Meeting of the American Psychological Association, Washington, D. C., 1967. Available from Dr. Robert F. Peterson, Department of Psychology, University of Illinois, Urbana, Illinois 61801.

Discusses advantages and problems involved in the use of behavior modification procedures and behavioral research that are carried out in the child's home.

31. Pumroy, D. K. A new approach to treating parent-child problems. Paper presented at the Annual Meeting of the American Psychological Association, Chicago, Illinois, 1965. Available from Dr. Donald K. Pumroy, Counseling Center, University of Maryland, College Park, Maryland 20740.

One of the early reports of consultative work with parents in training them to be the primary change agents in coping with behavior problems in their own children. The author worked with three groups: (1) parents of children in an elementary school; (2) parents of children in a day nursery; and (3) parents who had been referred to a mental hygiene clinic because of problems with their children. Of the eleven families that carried out the behavioral procedures, ten reported favorable results two months after the training sessions had concluded.

32. Pumroy, D. K. and Pumroy, S. S. *Modern child rearing: Behavioral principles applied to the raising of children.* Aldine-Atherton Publishers, 529 So. Wabash Ave., Chicago, Illinois 60605, 1972. In press.

This book was written with a two-fold purpose: (1) for students as supplementary reading in courses in child psychology; (2) for parents to help them understand and change the behaviors of their children. It would also be useful for teachers and student teachers. The book is divided into two major sections. Part One is concerned with a thorough description and explanation of the behavioral approach to child rearing including all of the associated principles and procedures (operant and respondent learning, positive and negative reinforcements, punishment, extinction, time-out, rules, tokens, contingency contracting, modeling, schedules of reinforcement, etc.). This section is replete with examples of child behaviors and problems with which parents attempt to cope in everyday life and provides helpful instructions for parents in the application of behavioral principles to these problems. Part Two of the book consists of six papers and published studies that illustrate the use of behavior modification in a variety of deviant or problem behaviors in children.

33. Rickard, H. C. and Mundy, M. B. Direct manipulation of stuttering behavior: An experimental-clinical approach. Available from Dr. Henry C. Rickard, Department of Psychology, University of Alabama, Tuscaloosa, Alabama 35486. Also in L. P. Ullman and L. P. Krasner (Eds.), *Case studies in behavior modification.* Holt, Rinehart and Winston, 383 Madison Ave., New York, New York 10017, 1965. Pp. 268-274 $11.50.

Report on the use of behavior modification in the outpatient treatment of stuttering in a nine-year-old boy. Stuttering behavior was ignored, while nonstuttering behavior was reinforced by praise and by means of a point system in which a given number of points could be exchanged for a desired object. Beginning with the eleventh session of the child with the mental health professional, the parents observed the reinforcement procedures and subsequently carried them out for nine sessions during a family vacation period. Considerable progress was made in decreasing the stuttering behavior of this boy, although a six-month follow-up indicated the gains had been only partially maintained.

34. Risley, T. R. and Wolf, M. M. Experimental manipulation of autistic behaviors and generalization into the home. Paper presented at the Annual Meeting of the American Psychological Association, Los Angeles, California, 1964. Available from Dr. Todd R. Risley, Turner House Preschool, Third and Stewart Sts., Kansas City, Kansas 66101. Also in S. W. Bijou and D. M. Baer (Eds.), *Child development: Readings in experimental analysis.* Appleton-Century-Crofts, 440 Park Ave., South, New York, New York 10016, 1967. Pp. 184-194 $4.50 paper.

One of the first reports on the use of parents as therapists. Describes a six-year-old autistic child who was echolalic and lacked other appropriate verbal behaviors. With training and consultation in the use of behavior modification by mental health professionals, the parents were able to contribute significantly to the improvement of their child's speech behavior in the home by continuing and extending gains initiated on an outpatient basis. The authors also refer to a similar program of parent training with seven sets of parents, all of whom carried out the major part of the behavior therapeutic process with their children in the home.

35. Russo, S. Adaptations in behavioral therapy with children. *Behaviour Research and Therapy,* 1964, *2,* 43-47. Available from Dr. Salvatore Russo, Children's Medical Center, Tulsa, Oklahoma 74105.

Discussion of the effective use of operant behavior modification procedures by two mothers involving a six-year-old girl and an eight-year-old boy, both of whom showed multiple behavior disturbances (aggressive, destructive, negativistic, etc.). On an outpatient basis, these mothers were trained by the mental health professional in the use of positive reinforcement for desirable and nonreinforcement of undesirable behaviors in their children. Substantial improvement resulted in both cases.

36. Shah, S. A. Training and utilizing a mother as the therapist for her child. Paper presented at the Annual Meeting of the Eastern Psychological Association, Boston, Massachusetts, 1967. Available from Dr. Saleem A. Shah, Center for Studies of Crime and Delinquency, National Institute of Mental Health, 5600 Fishers Lane, Rockville, Maryland 20852. Also in B. G. Guerney, Jr. (Ed.), *Psychotherapeutic agents: New roles for non-professionals, parents and teachers.* Holt, Rinehart and Winston, 383 Madison Ave., New York, New York 10017, 1969. Pp. 401-407 $10.50.

Discussion centers on working with the mother, herself emotionally disturbed, of a four-year-old girl with multiple behavior problems including enuresis, aggressive and destructive acts, etc. The mother-daughter relationship was extremely negative and mutually punitive.

Using a behavior modification framework, the mental health consultant worked exclusively with the mother in helping her learn how to apply operant reinforcement in decreasing undesirable and increasing desirable behavior in her daughter. The mother was successful in carrying out the "therapy process" and a follow-up about two years later showed that the improvement had lasted. In addition, this mother and daughter came to like and love each other, an experience previously unknown to them.

37. Smith, J. M. and Smith, D. E. P. *Child management: A program for parents.* Ann Arbor Publishers, 610 S. Forest Street, Ann Arbor, Michigan 48104, 1966. 97 pp. $3.00 paper, $4.50 hard.

A self-instructional manual and guide for parents, teachers, and others who deal with children. Although based on some aspects of operant conditioning, there is an absence of academic or theoretical discussions. Instead, the material is organized in terms of 176 problem situations involving: tantrums, enforcement of rules, eating, sleeping, tasks and responsibilities, development of independence, etc. The emphasis is on parental consistency, the use and enforcement of rules, and ignoring irrelevant or inappropriate behaviors.

38. Stuart, R. B. Behavioral contracting within the families of delinquents. Paper presented at the Annual Meeting of the American Psychological Association, Miami Beach, Florida, 1970. Available from Dr. Richard B. Stuart, School of Social Work, University of Michigan, Ann Arbor, Michigan 48104.

Concerned with the use of the Behavioral Contract, i.e., a written agreement that specifies exchangeable positive reinforcements based on privileges and responsibilities of parents and their delinquent offsprings. The contract involves explicit statements of privileges, responsibilities, reciprocities, sanctions and bonuses, means of monitoring the agreement, etc. The successful use of the contract as the primary treatment procedure is illustrated in the case of a sixteen-year-old delinquent girl and her parents.

39. Tahmisian, J. A. and McReynolds, W. T. Use of parents as behavioral engineers in the treatment of a school-phobic girl. *Journal of Counseling Psychology*, 1971, *18*, 225-228. Available from Dr. William T. McReynolds, Department of Psychology, University of Kentucky, Lexington, Kentucky 40506.

Report on a thirteen-year-old girl whose fear of going to school had resulted in her missing 80 consecutive days of school; psychiatric therapy, tranquilizers, as well as systematic desensitization had been tried without success. Behavior modification in the form of operant reinforcement, behavior-shaping, school-approach procedures were, however, successfully carried out by the parents who received consultative training from a mental health professional. The total treatment time was three weeks and involved only two hours of the professional's time—90 minutes for instructing and training the parents and ten minutes for each of three subsequent follow-up phone calls.

40. Wagner, M. K. Parent therapists: An operant conditioning method. *Mental Hygiene*, 1968, *52*. 452-455. Available from Dr. Mervyn K. Wagner, Department of Psychology, University of South Carolina, Columbia, South Carolina 29202.

Discusses the procedures involved in an outpatient setting in which parents are trained to carry out behavior modification therapy with their own children. A specific case is used to illustrate the process, and an outline guide of reinforcement procedures for parents is included.

41. Wahler, R. G., Winkel, G. H., Peterson, R. E., and Morrison, D. C. Mothers as behavior therapists for their own children. *Behaviour Research and Therapy,* 1965, *3*, 113-124. Available from Dr. Robert G. Wahler, Department of Psychology, University of Tennessee, Knoxville, Tennessee 37916. Also in B. G. Guerney, Jr. (Ed.), *Psychotherapeutic agents: New roles for non-professionals, parents and teachers.* Holt, Rinehart and Winston, 383 Madison Ave., New York, New York 10017, 1969. Pp. 519-533 $10.50.

Deviant behaviors in three children were modified by producing specific changes in the behaviors of their mothers which, in turn, produced marked changes in the children. With mental health consultation these mothers were able effectively to carry out behavior modification procedures with their own children. For a related and more recent discussion of how parents can learn how to use behavior modification procedures with children who have strong oppositional behaviors, see Wahler, R. G. Oppositional children: A quest for parental reinforcement control. *Journal of Applied Behavior Analysis*, 1969, *2*, 159-170.

42. Walder, L. O., Cohen, S. I., Breiter, D. E., Warman, F. C., Orme-Johnson, D., and Pavey, S. *Parents as agents of behavior change.* Behavior Service Consultants, Box 186, Greenbelt, Maryland 20770, 1971. 56 pp. $4.20 mimeographed.

Discusses results of work with over 50 families in which the parents of children with a variety of deviant behaviors were helped to "treat" their own children through an operant consultation system. Results were generally positive and led the authors to conclude that this kind of parental consultation approach could make a substantial contribution to meeting the mental health manpower problem by helping those who are most closely involved with children (i.e., parents) to do a better job.

43. Wetzel, R. J., Baker, J., Roney, M., and Martin, M. Outpatient treatment of autistic behavior. *Behaviour Research and Therapy,* 1966, *4,* 169-177. Available from Dr. R. J. Wetzel, Department of Psychology, University of Arizona, Tucson, Arizona 85721.

Report on the use of behavior modification by the parents of a six-year-old autistic boy who had frequent tantrums, who would often hit himself, whose speech was largely echolalic, etc. This boy and his parents were seen on a University Clinic outpatient basis, for 45-minute sessions twice weekly for three months. Mental health consultation by two graduate students, including home visits, enabled the parents to learn the effective use of reinforcement contingencies to decrease autistic and increase desirable behaviors in their son.

44. Williams, C. D. The elimination of tantrum behavior by extinction procedures. *Journal of Abnormal and Social Psychology,* 1959, *59,* 269. Available from Dr. Carl D. Williams, 9250 S.W. 81st Ave., Miami, Florida 33156.

Case of a 21-month-old boy who had been ill much of the first 18 months of his life and who continued to demand the special care and attention received during this time; tantrums and tyrannical behaviors were his way of controlling his parents, particularly at nap time and bedtime. The parents were counseled to withdraw all reinforcement (attention, talking, etc.) after putting the boy down for sleep. Within a matter of days, the deviant behaviors had been eliminated and a follow-up two years later showed him to be a friendly, outgoing child.

45. Wittes, G. and Radin, N. *The reinforcement approach: Helping your child to learn.* Dimensions Publishing Co., San Rafael, California 94903, 1969. 51 pp. $1.50 paper.

A handbook written specifically for parents and based on the author's training program in Ypsilanti, Michigan, involving six once-a-week sessions with groups of parents during which they learned how to apply behavioral principles with their own children. The material is organized in terms of six sections or "lessons" that cover a variety of situations, examples, and illustrations of operant reinforcement procedures with children. Each lesson includes home assignments and exercises for parents to complete with the emphasis being on specific child behaviors. This handbook would be helpful for mental health workers in counseling work with parents relative to both normal and deviant developmental behaviors in children. There are also two other related handbooks by the same authors: *The nurturance approach: Helping your child to learn* and *The learning through play approach: Helping your child to learn,* each of which is available, $1.50. For an outline and description of the Ypsilanti, Michigan, Parent Training and Education project, see Wittes, G. Parent Manual on Child Rearing: Unit I—Behavior Modification, 1968, mimeographed. Available from Dr. Glorianne Wittes, School of Social Work, University of Michigan, Ann Arbor, Michigan 48104.

46. Zeilberger, J., Sampsen, S. E., and Sloane, H. N., Jr. Modification of a child's problem behaviors in the home with the mother as therapist. *Journal of Applied Behavior Analysis*, 1968, *1*, 47-53. Available from Dr. Howard N. Sloane, Jr., Bureau of Educational Research, University of Utah, Salt Lake City, Utah 84112.

The case of a four-and-a-half-year-old boy with deviant behaviors including screaming, fighting, kicking, hitting, demanding, and related destructive behaviors. This boy's college-educated parents had been unable to manage him and had been told by the family doctor that his behavior reflected "a severe emotional problem." The mother was instructed in how to use systematic reinforcement contingencies and time-out procedures in the home to bring about marked decreases in destructive, and increases in desirable, behaviors.

47. Zifferblatt, S. M. *Improving study and homework behaviors.* Research Press, Box 3177 Country Fair Station, Champaign, Illinois 61820, 1970. 96 pp. $3.00 paper.

This manual was written to help parents learn how to positively manage their children's home behavior, particularly school work and learning. Although written in a completely nontechnical manner with a liberal use of drawings, a minimum of discussion, and no references, this material is based on several procedures in behavior modification work including: reinforcement, immediacy, sequencing, consistency, etc., and includes several examples of applications to problem situations. Could be used as an adjunct in counseling by professionals in mental health and education in working with parents.

Applications with Teachers   **2**

48. Ackerman, J. M. *Operant conditioning techniques for the classroom teacher.* Scott, Foresman & Co., Glenview, Illinois 60025, 1972. 143 pp. $2.75 paper.

Intended as a practical guide for teachers in learning behavior modification procedures for changing student behavior in classroom and other school settings. Key concepts and techniques are explained in terms of concrete examples including: initiating behavior changes, contingencies of reinforcement, token economies, shaping, priming, the Premack Principle, grades as reinforcers, punishment, use of peer groups, etc. This material would be helpful as a basic reference in consultative and inservice training work with teachers, special education teachers, and other school personnel.

49. Adams, D. H. The Ed White experience—Behavior modification in the public school. Paper ,prepared for presentation at the First Annual Symposium, Current Issues in Community-Clinical Psychology: School Intervention, March, 1971, University of Maryland, College Park, Maryland. Available from Dr. Daun. H. Adams, Huntsville-Madison County Mental Health Center, 218 Randolph Ave., Huntsville, Alabama 35801.

Report of a training program, offered by the local community mental health center for 30 teachers in a public junior high school in Huntsville, Alabama. The program conducted by Dr. Adams, a mental health consultant, involved one pretraining and six group training sessions that covered basic principles and applications of behavior modification. Fifteen problem students were identified by the teachers and successful interventions carried out using behavioral procedures. The overall evaluation of this program was quite positive and demonstrated how two community agencies, i.e., public school system and mental health center, can work together in making significant contributions to child and school mental health.

50. Allen, K. E., Turner, K. D., and Everett, P. M. A behavior modification classroom for Head Start children with behavior problems. *Exceptional Children*, 1970, *37*, 119-129. Available from Dr. K. Eileen Allen, 143 Experimental Education Unit, Child Development and Retardation Center, WJ-110, University of Washington, Seattle, Washington 98105.

Describes a demonstration and training project in which 12 to 15 preschool children with behavioral problems were enrolled in a special Head Start class. The goals of the project were to: (1) demonstrate the effectiveness of behavior modification procedures in reducing or eliminating deviant behaviors, and increasing desirable behaviors in these children; (2) provide Head Start teachers and related personnel with inservice training in behavior modification procedures; and (3) do applied research based on the behavioral analyses of teacher-child interactions. Case studies of two of the children are presented together with an outline-discussion of behavioral principles and techniques relevant to these cases. For related papers of the senior author, see Allen, K. E. The behavior modification approach to pre-school education. Paper presented at a meeting of Head Start Regional Training Officers and Directors, Seattle, Washington, 1969; and Allen, K. E. The application of behavior modification principles to the learning deficits of handicapped preschool children. Paper presented at a Special Study Institute for Directors of Exemplary Early Childhood Centers for Handicapped Children, Rougemont, North Carolina, 1970.

51. Axelrod, S. Token reinforcement programs in special classes. *Exceptional Children*, 1971, *37*, 371-379. Available from Dr. Saul Axelrod, Department of Educational Psychology, University of Connecticut, Storrs, Connecticut 06268.

Reviews the use of token reinforcement systems in a number of studies of special education classes involving: (1) increasing school skills in mentally and educationally retarded children, teenagers with multiple handicaps, adolescent school dropouts, underachieving children from urban poverty areas, emotionally disturbed children, and those with various learning disabilities; and (2) decreasing various disruptive, maladaptive, and other deviant behaviors. The author reports positive results were obtained in all of these studies despite the variety of target behaviors and different kinds of children involved. The suggestion is made that future studies can make greater use of natural reinforcements in the child's everyday environment including those existing in classroom and other school settings.

52. Baer, D. M. and Wolf, M. M. The reinforcement contingency in preschool and remedial education. In R. D. Hess and R. M. Baer (Eds.), *Early Education*. Aldine Publishers, 529 S. Wabash, Chicago, Illinois 60605, 1968. Pp. 119-129 $7.50.

Concerned with the application of behavior modification procedures by teachers to young children with various behavior problems including regressive crawling, frequent crying, social isolation, overdependency, aggression, negativism, etc. Discusses the fundamental role of operant reinforcement in the development, maintenance, and modification of child behavior problems.

53. Becker, W. C. (Ed.) *An empirical basis for change in education: Selections on behavioral psychology for teachers.* Science Research Associates, 259 East Erie St., Chicago, Illinois 60611, 1971. 522 pp. $5.95 paper.

This is a collection of 36 readings selected to supplement courses in the training of teachers in the use of behavior modification procedures. Examples of the variety of topics and kinds of applications covered include: reducing behavior problems in the classroom; the use of token systems; increasing academic skills in low achievers; behavioral approaches to tantrums, school phobias, aggression, etc.; inservice teacher training program in contingency management; individually prescribed and programmed systems of instruction, etc. This book of readings would be helpful as a supplementary reference in courses in educational psychology, child development for teachers, special education, school mental health, etc.

54. Becker, W. C., Engelmann, S., and Thomas, D. R. *Teaching: A course in applied psychology.* Science Research Associates, 259 East Erie St., Chicago, Illinois 60611, 1971. 499 pp. $6.95 paper; Teacher's Guide, $2.00 paper.

This book was written as a workbook-type text for the training of classroom teachers in the use of behavior modification principles and procedures in school settings. The first half is a behavior modification primer for teachers, while the second half is concerned with teaching conceptual learning and directed tasks plus several concluding chapters on implications and applications for problem-solving, programming, handicapped children, and changes in the educative process. The material is well organized, clearly presented, and replete with illustrations and demonstrations of the effective use of operant reinforcement, setting up a token system, Premack Principle, punishment and time-out, etc. Each chapter is followed by exercises.

55. Becker, W. C., Thomas, D. R., and Carnine, D. *Reducing behavior problems: An operant conditioning guide for teachers.* Educational Resources Information Center, University of Illinois, 805 W. Pennsylvania Ave., Urbana, Illinois 61801, 1969. 37 pp. $1.65 paper.

Concepts, principles, and procedures of operant reinforcement learning are clearly set forth and discussed in terms of preschool-age children. A considerable amount of work during the past several years is summarized involving behavior modification in decreasing disruptive and other deviant behaviors and in increasing desirable behavior in both preschool and school-age children. For an earlier report on training five teachers in behavior modification procedures (ignoring deviant and reinforcing productive behaviors) involving five classes in a public elementary school with 95% black children, see Becker, W. C., Madsen, C. H., Jr., Arnold, C. R., and Thomas, D. R. The contingent use of teacher attention and praise in reducing class-room behavior problems. *Journal of Special Education*, 1967, *1*, 287-307. Available from Dr. Wesley C. Becker, Department of Special Education, University of Oregon, Eugene, Oregon 97403.

56. Benson, F. A. M. (Ed.) *Modifying deviant social behaviors in various classroom settings*. Department of Special Education, College of Education, University of Oregon, Eugene, Oregon 97403, 1969. 80 pp. $2.15 paper.

This monograph consists of two major sections: one, by G. R. Patterson, D. A. Shaw, and M. J. Ebner, concerned with the use of behavior modification with teachers, peers, and parents as agents of change in the classroom; and the other, by H. M. Walker, R. H. Mattson, and N. K. Buckley, concerned with a study of the use of behavior modification procedures in a special classroom placement of 12 boys, grades four to six, all with multiple deviant behaviors (defiance, hyperactivity, distractibility, tantrum outbursts, etc.). There are discussions of various principles and applications to a variety of child mental health and educational-behavioral problems.

57. Bergan, J. R. and Caldwell, T. Operant techniques in school psychology. *Psychology in the Schools*, 1967, *4*, 136-141. Available from Dr. John R. Bergan, Department of Educational Psychology, College of Education, University of Arizona, Tucson, Arizona 85721.

A discussion of the school psychologist as a behavior modification consultant to teachers. Refers to Lindsley's survey of those classroom problems with which teachers need help. About 62 percent were deceleration type problems, i.e., behaviors to be reduced or eliminated; while 32 percent were acceleration problems, i.e., behaviors to be developed or increased. About three-fourths of problems of all kinds involved boys in contrast to girls.

58. Bradfield, R. H. (Ed.) *Behavior modification: The human effort.* Dimensions Publishing Co., San Rafael, California 94903, 1970. 218 pp. $4.95 paper.

The focus of this book, which includes contributions of a number of outstanding workers in the field, is on the principles and applications of behavior modification to the education of different groups of children: normal, gifted, disturbed, handicapped, etc. Such topics or subjects as the following are included: the steps involved in behavioral analysis, training behavior analysts, the engineered classroom, language acquisition, reading improvement, thinking skills through behavioral programming, and applications to disadvantaged and psychotic children. In addition, there is a section on various issues in behavior modification, e.g., moral and ethical considerations, criticisms and resistances, research and application, etc. For a discussion of the behavior modification approach in teaching developed by Lindsley and others, see Bradfield, R. H. Precision teaching: A useful technology for special education teachers. *Educational Technology*, 1970, *10*, 22-26. Available from Dr. R. H. Bradfield, Department of Special Education, San Francisco State College, San Francisco, California 94132.

59. Broden, M., Hall, R. V., Dunlap, A., and Clark, R. Effects of teacher attention and a token reinforcement system in a junior high school special education class. *Exceptional Children*, 1970, *36*, 341-349. Available from Dr. R. Vance Hall, Bureau of Child Research, Juniper Gardens Children's Project, 2021 North Third, Kansas City, Kansas 66101.

A study of 13 seventh and eighth grade students, enrolled in a junior high school special class—eight boys and five girls—all with multiple behavior problems, marked academic retardation, and related handicaps. With consultative assistance from mental health workers, the teacher, who was in her first year of teaching, learned how to use behavior modification procedures in markedly decreasing deviant behaviors and increasing productive behaviors. Although attending to study and ignoring nonstudy classroom behaviors on the part of the teacher significantly increased study behaviors, the use of a timer and, later, a point contingency system with backup desirable reinforcements were particularly effective both in eliminating most of the disruptive behaviors and increasing school achievement and positive adjustment.

60. Brown, P. and Elliott, R. Control of aggression in a nursery school class. *Journal of Experimental Child Psychology*, 1965, *2*, 103-107. Available from Dr. Rogers Elliott, Department of Psychology, Dartmouth College, Hanover, New Hampshire 03755.

Study of 27 three- and four-year-old boys in a nursery school in which the frequency and extent of aggressive behaviors were successfully reduced by the teacher carrying out systematic application of the behavior modification procedures involving nonreinforcement of aggressive and reinforcement of cooperative, nonaggressive behaviors.

61. Buckley, N. K. and Walker, H. M. *Modifying classroom behavior.* Research Press, Box 3177 Country Fair Station, Champaign, Illinois 61820, 1970. 124 pp. $4.00 paper.

Written as a practical, semi-programmed manual for teachers and student teachers in the use of behavior modification principles and procedures in the classroom. Covers various aspects including reinforcement, modeling, shaping, extinction, punishment, time-out, etc. Could be used as an adjunct in consultative work with teachers.

62. Bushell, D., Jr. and Brigham, T. A. Classroom token systems as technology. *Educational Technology*, 1971, *11*, 14-17. Available from Dr. Don Bushell, Jr., Department of Human Development, University of Kansas, Lawrence, Kansas 66044.

A discussion of the development, advantages, effectiveness, and present status of token reinforcement systems in classroom settings. The authors refer to the current use of behavior analysis and token systems in some 200 classrooms—preschool through third grade— throughout the country involved in Project Follow Through for children from poor, deprived backgrounds. In this connection, a guide has been prepared for setting up a token system in classrooms, A Token Manual for Behavior Analysis Classrooms, that may be obtained from: Follow Through, Department of Human Development, University of Kansas, Lawrence, Kansas 66044.

63. Carter, R. D. *Help! These kids are driving me crazy*. Research Press, Box 3177 Country Fair Station, Champaign, Illinois 61820, 1972. 112 pp. $2.75 paper.

This manual was written for the classroom teacher in learning to apply behavior modification procedures to establish and maintain classroom management, to decrease unproductive behaviors, and to facilitate desirable behaviors in students. The material is presented in a novel, nonacademic, easily understandable manner and includes many helpful examples, guidelines, and suggestions for implementing effective reinforcement systems in classroom settings. Would be helpful in consultative and inservice training work with both elementary and secondary school teachers.

64. Chan, A., Chin, A., and Mueller, D. J. An integrated approach to the modification of classroom failure and disruption: A case study. *Journal of School Psychology*, 1970, *8*, 114-121. Available from Dr. Adrian Chan, Department of Educational Psychology, University of Wisconsin-Milwaukee, Milwaukee, Wisconsin 53201.

Report on the successful use of behavior modification with an eleven-year-old black boy with various disruptive behaviors and academic failure in a predominately white, middle class, elementary school. Behavioral and counseling approaches including remedial assistance, peer involvement, and teacher training were utilized. The concept of "therapeutic education" is discussed in relation to this study.

65. Davis, M., Morris, J., and Price, G. Token reinforcement programs in the public school. Paper presented at the Annual Meeting of the Rocky Mountain Psychological Association, Salt Lake City, Utah, 1970. Available from Dr. Michael Davis, Department of Psychology, University of Utah, Salt Lake City, Utah 84112.

Reports on the use of operant reinforcement programs in two public school classes, third and sixth grades. Two major behavioral contingencies, positive and negative, were used involving a token and point system to increase desired behaviors and academic achievement and to decrease disruptive behaviors, classroom noise levels, etc. Results demonstrated the practicability and effectiveness of these behavior modification procedures in a public school setting with classes having 30 or more pupils.

66. Dee, V. Contingency management in a crisis class. Prepublication paper, 1971. Available from Mrs. Verita Dee, 8241 North Central Ave., Phoenix, Arizona 85020.

Describes a special class for children with emotional problems in the Scottsdale School District, Arizona. The program and procedures of this "Crisis Class" are based on a behavior modification model with special emphasis on the Premack Principle and the work of Homme and others, i.e., low probability behaviors (doing class assignments, observing classroom rules, academic achievement, etc.) may be increased if high probability behaviors (recess, sports, play activities, etc.) are contingent on the prior occurrence of the low probability behaviors. The author describes the procedures she used in this class, reviews the cases of two children as illustrations of the extent that behavioral change is possible, and concludes with an outline-recipe for using the Contingency Management System which, on the basis of her experience, she readily recommends.

67. Dickinson, D. J. Changing behavior with behavioral techniques. *Journal of School Psychology*, **1968, 6, 278-283. Available from Dr. Donald J. Dickinson, Coordinator of Special Student Services, Clark County School District, Las Vegas, Nevada 89109.**

A behavior modification program was carried out with an eight-year-old boy in a third grade class of 36 children. This boy showed a variety of disruptive and unproductive behaviors in the classroom including being out of his seat, talking without permission, throwing things, hitting others, failure to complete school assignments, hiding from the teacher, etc. This teacher received training in the use of operant reinforcement procedures and within a period of several days was able to bring about marked improvement in this boy's school behaviors.

68. Dyer, V. An example: Reinforcement principles in a classroom for emotionally disturbed children. *Exceptional Children*, 1968, *34*, 597-599. Available from Mrs. Verita Dee, 8241 North Central Ave., Phoenix, Arizona 85020.

Describes the behavioral and academic rehabilitation of an emotionally disturbed, twelve-and-one-half-year-old girl through the use of behavior modification procedures. This girl was withdrawn, aloof, depressed, and unable to do her school work. A token system was used to accelerate appropriate social behavior, while direct, "M & M"—type reinforcement was used for academic achievement. Marked improvement was obtained over a period of several months in a special education and day treatment program.

69. *Educational Technology,* 1971, *11.* Educational Technology Publications, Inc., 140 Sylvan Ave., Englewood Cliffs, New Jersey 07632. $3.95 (April Issue).

This special issue is concerned with a representative sampling of some of the important applications of behavior modification and, specifically, the use of contingency management within educational settings. Includes a series of 14 papers that cover such topics as contingency management in university courses and in correctional institutions; use of token systems and punishment in the classroom; training teachers in the use of contingency management; workshop in behavior modification for elementary school teachers, self-instructional systems; and applications for children with academic, speech, and social adjustment problems. The material contained in this issue would be useful in inservice training and consultative work with teachers.

70. *Exceptional Children*, 1970, *37.* The Council for Exceptional Children, Jefferson Plaza, Suite 900, Arlington, Virginia 22202. $1.50 (October Issue).

This entire issue is concerned with behavior modification and includes such topics as: (1) a review of the brief history and a contemporary analysis of behavior modification with exceptional children; (2) application to: (a) severely language-handicapped children, (b) classroom problem behaviors, (c) Head Start children with behavior problems, (d) precision teaching and teacher-pupil inter-actions; (3) training teachers as behavioral consultants in classroom management; (4) future directions of the behavioral model in child and school mental health work.

71. Fargo, G. A., Behrns, C., and Nolen, P. (Eds.) *Behavior modification in the classroom*. Wadsworth Publishing Co., Belmont, California 94002, 1970. 344 pp. $4.95 paper.

This is a collection of 39 articles, most of which were previously published, designed primarily for teachers and student teachers concerned with classroom management. Some of the major topics include: ethical and theoretical issues in behavior modification; the normal preschool and elementary school classroom; the special classroom for emotionally disturbed, mentally retarded, academically disabled, and disadvantaged children; language and speech therapy; and parents as therapists. Would be suitable as supplementary reading in college or inservice education courses for teachers.

72. Fine, M. J. Some qualifying notes on the development and implementation of behavior modification programs. *Journal of School Psychology*, 1970, *8*, 301-305. Available from Dr. Marvin J. Fine, School Psychology Training Program, School of Education, University of Kansas, Lawrence, Kansas 66044.

A brief discussion of value judgments in the use of behavior modification procedures in school settings with emphasis on: (1) both pre- and post-environmental contingency arrangements, (2) the student's involvement in the behavior modification program, and (3) dealing with both the resistances and over responsiveness of teachers to the use of behavior modification in classrooms.

73. Goodwin, D. L. Training a school staff in behavior modification: A systems approach. Paper presented at the Annual Meeting of the Western Psychological Association, Vancouver, British Columbia, 1969. Available from Dr. Dwight L. Goodwin, Department of Psychology, San Jose State College, San Jose, California 95114.

A report concerned with the introduction and establishment of the behavior modification model within the school system of the Santa Clara, California, Unified School District. Includes discussion of consultation with school administrators and applications of behavioral procedures in working with teachers, i.e., analysis and reinforcement of the behaviors of teachers as well as training teachers in the use of behavioral techniques with children in school settings. This report covers the first year of an ongoing project (a report based on the completed project, involving twenty selected school districts throughout California was completed in 1972 and is available from Dr. Dwight L. Goodwin at the above address).

74. Goodwin, D. L., Garvey, W. P., and Barclay, J. R. Microconsultation and behavior analysis: A method of training psychologists as behavioral consultants. *Journal of Consulting and Clinical Psychology*,

1971, *37*, 355-363. Available from Dr. Dwight L. Goodwin, Department of Psychology, San Jose State College, San Jose, California 95114.

Describes and discusses the experimental evaluation of a training procedure, termed microconsultation, for instructing school psychologists in a set of interview skills for using behavior modification with teachers. An eight-week summer workshop for experienced school psychologists was carried out with a group of 30 randomly selected trainees, and their subsequent work performance was compared to two control groups with significant improvement in the predicted direction. The microconsultation procedure—which consists of a series of brief face-to-face practice, videotaped sessions that enable the trainee to acquire specific skills in a naturalistic setting—involves several important aspects of learning including feedback, shaping by staff and fellow trainees, and imitation modeling. The authors conclude that in terms of effectiveness, efficiency, and economy, the microconsultation training model has many advantages over traditional approaches.

75. Grieger, R. M., II. Behavior modification with a total class: A case report. *Journal of School Psychology*, 1970, *8*, 103-106. Available from Dr. Russell M. Grieger, II, Child Study Center, 65 South Oval Dr., Ohio State University, Columbus, Ohio 43210.

Reports on the successful use of behavior modification in a class of nine children, ages eight to eleven, all of average intelligence but achieving at least one year below the expected level. Four teachers (reading, arithmetic, arts, and crafts) carried out the project using a combination of social, material, and token reinforcement systems to reduce various disruptive behaviors and increase positive classroom work. For a review of important factors in establishing and providing consultation relative to behavior modification programs in schools including training of teachers, see Grieger, R. M., II, Mordock, J. B., and Breyer, N. General guidelines for conducting behavior modification programs in public school settings. *Journal of School Psychology*, 1970, *8*, 259-266.

76. Hall, R. V., Panyan, M., Rabon, D., and Broden, M. Instructing beginning teachers in reinforcement procedures which improve classroom control. *Journal of Applied Behavior Analysis*, 1968, *1*, 315-322. Available from Dr. R. Vance Hall, Bureau of Child Research, Juniper Gardens Children's Project, 2021 North Third, Kansas City, Kansas 66101.

Reports on consultation to three beginning teachers (first, sixth, and seventh grades) who had experienced difficulty maintaining classroom control, teaching satisfactorily, etc. These teachers learned how to use systematic reinforcement procedures and were able to bring about marked improvements in class management, study behaviors in students, etc. The authors conclude that behavior modification procedures can be carried out by teachers in classrooms with little or no added expense and without major administrative changes. For a suggested course or workshop to train teachers to carry out behavior modification procedures, see Hall, R. V. Training teachers in classroom use of contingency management. *Educational Technology*, 1971, *11*, 33-38. See also Hall, R.V. and Copeland, R. E. The responsive teaching model: A first step in shaping school personnel as behavior modification specialists. Paper presented at the Third Banff International Conference on Behavior Modification, Calgary, Alberta, Canada, 1971. In F. W. Clark, D. R. Evans, and L. A. Hamerlynck (Eds.), *Implementing behavioral programs for schools and clinics*. Research Press Company, Box 3177 Country Fair Station, Champaign, Illinois 61820, 1972. Pp. 125-138 $4.00 paper.

77. Haring, N. G. and Hauck, M. A. Improved learning conditions in the establishment of reading skills with disabled readers. *Exceptional Children*, 1969, *35*, 341-352. Available from Dr. Norris G. Haring, Experimental Education Unit, Child Development and Retardation Center, University of Washington, Seattle, Washington 98105.

Report on the use of a token reinforcement system with four elementary school boys (grades 3, 4, 4, and 5) all of whom were of normal intelligence, but severely disabled in reading. The token system involved points, and later marbles, which were exchangeable for edibles, trinkets, and other more expensive items of known reinforcing value to these boys. Individually programmed, sequentially-arranged reading materials were used with token reinforcements to accelerate performance rate and, subsequently, to maintain the high rate. Progress in reading over a five-month token reinforcement period ranged from one-and-one-half to four-year levels. For a related discussion, see Haring, N. G. The systematic use of contingencies in classes for children with academic and social response deficits. *Educational Technology*, 1971, *11*, 54-58.

78. Haring, N. G. and Lovitt, T. C. Operant methodology and educational technology in special education. In N. G. Haring and R. L. Schiefelbusch (Eds.), *Methods in special education*. McGraw-Hill Book Co., 330 West 42nd St., New York, New York 10036, 1967. Pp. 12-48 $8.95.

A review of studies and applied research concerned with the use and methodology of operant behavior modification by teachers in special education work with exceptional children, ranging from preschool to high school age, and including children who were autistic, culturally deprived, educationally or mentally retarded, neurologically impaired, potential school dropouts, etc. The authors suggest that the establishment of the behavior modification model in special education work with children provides a basis for the teacher carrying out a more active role in the mental health as well as educational development of children. For a discussion of the application of behavior modification procedures with disturbed and other handicapped children in preschool settings, see Haring, N. G., Hayden, A. H., and Allen, K. E. Intervention in early childhood. *Educational Technology*, 1971, *11*, 52-61. Available from Dr. Norris G. Haring, Experimental Education Unit, Child Development and Retardation Center, University of Washington, Seattle, Washington 98105.

79. Harman, R., Gelfand, D. M., and Nielsen, E. Token economy to control disruptive behavior in a regular sixth grade classroom. Paper presented at the Annual Meeting of the Western Psychological Association, Los Angeles, California, 1970. Available from Dr. Donna Gelfand, Department of Psychology, University of Utah, Salt Lake City, Utah 84112.

Report of the successful use of a reinforcement token system by the teacher in effectively reducing disruptive behavior in a sixth grade class of 33 students, ages eleven to thirteen. Tokens with back-up reinforcers (e.g., extra recess, movie, arts and crafts, etc.) were based on preferences of the students and were used both on an individual and group basis for increasing appropriate behaviors.

80. Harris, M. B. *Classroom uses of behavior modification*. Charles E. Merrill Publishing Co., 1300 Alum Creek Dr., Columbus, Ohio 43216, 1972. $5.95 paper.

This volume consists of six sections, the first two of which are concerned with basic principles, implementation, and evaluation of applications of behavior modification within school settings. The next three sections consist of 23 papers and reports of studies to: (1) increase certain classroom behaviors, (2) decrease certain classroom behaviors, and (3) reinforcement programs in various educational programs. The final section has eight papers concerned with practical implications and issues including training teachers and teacher aides in behavior modification procedures, ethical considerations, etc. This book, designed for students and workers in psychology and education, practicing teachers, etc., would be useful in inservice courses for teachers and others concerned with the education of children and youth.

81. Hawkins, R. P., McArthur, M., Rinaldi, P. C., and Gray, D. Results of operant conditioning techniques in modifying the behavior of emotionally disturbed children. Paper presented at the Annual Meeting of the International Council for Exceptional Children, St. Louis,

Missouri, 1967. Available from Dr. Robert P. Hawkins, Department of Psychology, Western Michigan University, Kalamazoo, Michigan 49001.

Describes an experimental public school program based on behavior modification procedures for emotionally disturbed children. This program included two special classrooms, called School-Adjustment Classrooms, as well as provision for treatment of individual children in regular classrooms. A total of eleven children (seven boys and four girls), ages eight to eleven, were enrolled in the School-Adjustment Classes; these classes were conducted by teaching staff who had been given inservice training in principles and procedures in behavior modification and graduate students in psychology and education. The effectiveness of the overall program is discussed and the progress of two other children, treated with behavior modification procedures in regular classes, is described. See also the senior author's paper, The school adjustment program: Individualized intervention with children with behavior disorders. Presented at Second Annual Kansas Symposium on Behavior Analysis in Education, University of Kansas, Lawrence, Kansas, 1971.

82. Hewett, F. M. *The emotionally disturbed child in the classroom.* Allyn and Bacon, 470 Atlantic Ave., Boston, Massachusetts 02110, 1968. 373 pp. $9.95.

A text written for classroom teachers to help them understand and teach children who have learned various maladaptive behaviors that interfere with their social adjustment and academic achievement. Based on 15 years experience in working with emotionally disturbed children in both clinical and school settings, the author presents his "Developmental Sequence of Educational Goals" which is based on those essential behaviors and competencies that all children need in order to successfully learn in school; the requisites on the part of the child include: paying attention, responding, following directions, exploring the environment, relating to peers, mastering self-care behaviors, achieving academic goals, and self-motivation for further learning. Operant reinforcement is a major component in the author's approach. Approximately the last third of the book is devoted to a comprehensive description of the "Engineered Classroom," a specially designed, school-learning environment, and the Santa Monica School Project— both developed to maximize the attainment of developmental educational goals for disturbed and other handicapped children.

83. Hewett, F. M., Taylor, F. D., and Artuso, A. A. The Santa Monica Project: Evaluation of an engineered classroom design with emotionally disturbed children. *Exceptional Children*, 1969, *35*, 523-529. Available from Dr. Frank M. Hewett, Department of Special Education, N-P Institute, UCLA, Los Angeles, California 90024.

Reports on a study of 54 children, eight to twelve years of age, all of whom had learning and behavioral problems. Six classrooms, with nine students in each, were used to compare the relative effectiveness of a behaviorally programmed approach in contrast to the usual classroom model as far as pupil attention, achievement, etc., were concerned. Overall results were favorable in increasing teacher effectiveness as a social reinforcer and for increasing certain behavioral competencies in school children.

84. Homme, L. E., et al. *How to use contingency contracting in the classroom.* Research Press, Box 3177 Country Fair Station, Champaign, Illinois 61820, 1969. 130 pp. $3.50 paper.

A programmed manual for teachers in applying principles of operant reinforcement learning to the classroom. Also includes sections on preparation of materials, classroom organization, management of the class, and the use of self-contracting in students.

85. Homme, L. E., de Baca, P. C., Devine, J. V., Steinhorst, R., and Rickert, E. J. Use of the Premack Principle in controlling the behavior of nursery school children. *Journal of the Experimental Analysis of Behavior,* 1963, *6,* 544. Available from Individual Learning Systems. P. O. Box 3388, San Rafael, California 94902.

A one-page report on the use of the Premack Principle with three three-year-old nursery school children relative to decreasing undesirable and increasing desirable behaviors. The authors demonstrated how high probability behaviors such as running around the room, pushing chairs, talking or screaming, etc., could be used to increase low probability behaviors such as sitting quietly in a chair, looking at the blackboard, listening to the teacher, etc. They concluded that application of this reinforcement principle was an exceptionally practical procedure for teachers in controlling the behavior of nursery school children.

86. James, R. E., Jr. *Behavior management systems associates: I. Student achievement record* and *II. Teacher's manual.* Behavior Management Systems, 311 South Grace St., Rocky Mount, North Carolina, 1971. $4.50 (Student's Record) and $5.00 (Teacher's Manual).

These two manuals constitute a classroom contingency management system to increase academic, prosocial, creative, and other specified desirable behaviors. The manual for teachers includes an outline of behavior modification principles and procedures, the use of written behavioral contracts, reinforcement menu for pupils, teacher's self-management, principal's involvement, home-school coordination, and steps in the implementation of a classroom behavior management system. The record for students includes weekly score cards; achievement contract forms for the specification of academic, prosocial, or other goals; points earned for each achievement; graphs for recording of progress; home-school coordination with guidelines for parents, home contingencies, etc. These manuals provide a basis for teachers learning to use a behavioral reinforcement program in their own classrooms.

87. Knowles, P. L., Prutsman, T. D., and Raduege, V. Behavior modification of simple hyperkinetic behavior and letter discrimination in a hyperactive child. *Journal of School Psychology*, 1968, *6*, 157-160. Available from Dr. Patsy Livingston, Florida Atlantic University, Boca Raton, Florida 33432.

Case of a seven-year-old boy with a Wechsler IQ of 116 who was repeating the first grade. This boy had two major problems that were pinpointed for modification: (1) he was extremely hyperactive most of the time, running through the halls at school, disrupting the classroom, etc.; and (2) he reversed letters in his writing. He had been given a medical diagnosis of "brain damage." On the basis of mental health consultation in the use of behavior modification procedures, the special education teacher was able to eliminate both the hyperactive behavior and letter reversals in writing.

88. Krumboltz, J. D. and Thoresen, C. E. (Eds.) *Behavioral counseling: Cases and techniques.* Holt, Rinehart & Winston, 383 Madison Ave., New York, New York 10017, 1969. 515 pp. $9.00.

A book of 43 readings and reports concerned with the use of behavior modification and related approaches with individuals having various kinds of mental health and school adjustment problems. Much of the content is directly relevant to applications of behavioral procedures in educational settings: elementary school, 14 readings; secondary school, 16 readings; and colleges-universities, 12 readings. Some of the major topics covered include: coping with deviant child behaviors, improving academic performance, study behaviors, social skills, eliminating fears of public speaking, use of behavioral contracts in teaching and counseling, behavioral consultation to teachers, etc. Suitable as a text and resource book for mental health professionals in consultative work and training programs for teachers, counselors, and personnel concerned with special education, school psychology, school nursing, school social work, and related services.

89. Kubany, E. S., Weiss, L. E., and Sloggett, B. B. The good behavior clock: A reinforcement/time out procedure for reducing disruptive classroom behavior. *Journal of Behavior Therapy and Experimental Psychiatry,* 1971, *2,* 173-179. Available from Dr. Edward S. Kubany, Department of Psychology, University of Hawaii, Honolulu, Hawaii 96822.

The authors report on the successful use of an innovative behavioral procedure that subantially decreased the extremely disruptive classroom behavior of a first-grade boy named Henry. The procedure, which combined positive reinforcement for desirable behavior (e.g., in-seat, task oriented, etc.) and time-out for undesirable behaviors (e.g., out-of-seat, hyperactivity, disturbing peers, etc.), consisted of a 15-minute electric timer, called "Henry's Clock," fitted with a special dial, placed on a desk in front of the room, and operated by the teacher. For every two minutes recorded by the clock, Henry earned one "treat"; these "treats" accumulated in a "Sharing Jar" which he shared with his classmates. This study suggests that classroom teachers can effectively cope with highly disruptive behaviors provided they are trained in the use of reinforcement procedures.

90. Kunzelmann, H. P. (Ed.) *Precision teaching: An initial training sequence.* Special Child Publications, Inc., 4535 Union Bay Place, N.E., Seattle, Washington 98105, 1970. 310 pp. $5.95 paper.

A programmed manual written specifically for classroom teachers by the editor and four teacher-colleagues, based on their classroom work with 40 children over a four-year period at an Experimental Education Unit of the University of Washington. The contents are an extension of the original work in behavior modification of Lindsley involving: (1) pinpointing behaviors, (2) recording the frequency and rate, (3) changing the contingencies affecting the behavior, and (4) trying again if the first effort is not effective. The emphasis is on the identification of target behaviors and the use of recording, counting, measuring, and charting techniques in the classroom. Suitable in teacher training and inservice courses for teachers.

91. Kuypers, D. S., Becker, W. C., and O'Leary, K. D. How to make a token system fail. *Exceptional Children*, 1968, *35*, 101-109. Available from Dr. Daniel S. Kuypers, 805 N. Gadsden, Tallahassee, Florida 32303.

A study of the use of a token system used in a special adjustment class of six third-grade and six fourth-grade children with multiple behavior problems (e.g., tantrums, fighting and other classroom disruptive behaviors, educational retardation, etc.). The purpose was to determine those factors that facilitate and those that interfere with the effective application of a token contingency system in the classroom. An outline is included of instructions and procedures to follow in setting up a token system along with discussion of specific problems that must be reckoned with in carrying out a successful program.

92. Lovitt, T. C., Guppy, T. E., and Blattner, J. E. The use of a free-time contingency with fourth graders to increase spelling accuracy. *Behaviour Research and Therapy*, 1969, *7*, 151-156. Available from Dr. Thomas C. Lovitt, Child Development and Mental Retardation Center, University of Washington, Seattle, Washington 98195.

Report on the use of contingent reinforcement procedures in a fourth grade class of 32 middle and upper middle class pupils in a public school. Increased accuracy in spelling was reinforced individually by pupil-selected, free time activity and on a group basis by radio listening. With back-up assistance and consultation, this successful endeavor was carried out entirely by the regular classroom teacher who administered the spelling program, recorded and graphed the pupils' scores, and managed the contingency system.

93. Madsen, C. H., Jr. and Madsen, C. K. *Teaching/discipline: Behavioral principles toward a positive approach.* **Allyn and Bacon, Inc., 470 Atlantic Ave., Boston, Massachusetts 02210, 1970. 139 pp. $2.95 paper.**

A manual and guide for teachers and prospective teachers in the use of behavior modification principles and procedures. Includes a series of 20 questions and answers (e.g., what is behavior modification? why don't students learn? etc.) and a selected sample of 55 scientific and professional examples of behavior changing practices applicable to classroom teaching situations (e.g., disruptive, out-of-control behaviors, boredom, apathy, low achievement and academic failures, nailbiting, noncooperative and socially withdrawn behaviors, etc.). Would be helpful in inservice work with teachers. For a report of an inservice training project in behavior modification conducted by mental health workers and college students for 32 elementary school teachers, see Madsen, C. H., Jr., Madsen, C. K., Saudagras, R. A., Hammond, W. R., and Smith, J. B. Classroom RAID (rules, approval, ignore, dissaproval): A cooperative approach for professionals and volunteers. *Journal of School Psychology*, 1970, *8*, 180-185. Available from Dr. Charles H. Madsen, Jr., Department of Psychology, Florida State University, Tallahassee, Florida 32306.

94. Meacham, M. L. The school psychologist: Classroom consultant in behavioral techniques. Paper presented at the Annual Meeting of the American Psychological Association, Washington, D. C., 1971. Available from Dr. Merle L. Meacham, Department of Special Education, University of Washington, Seattle, Washington 98105.

This paper, prepared for a symposium on Changing Teacher Behavior: Success and Failure with Behavior Modification in the Classroom, discusses two major roles of the school psychologist as a behavioral consultant to: (1) consultants, e.g., groups of counselors, school psychologists, principals, reading specialists, etc.; and (2) classroom teachers. The role of the behavioral school psychologist-consultant is discussed in terms of helping teachers function more effectively along with the success ratio of reducing maladaptive in relation to increasing academic behaviors, skills, etc., of children in the classroom. Three classroom teachers also presented papers at the above-indicated symposium concerned with reinforcements and non-reinforcements for teachers and behavior modification from the viewpoint of a classroom teacher.

95. Meacham, M. L. and Wiesen, A. E. *Changing classroom behavior: A manual for precision teaching.* International Textbook Co., Scranton, Pennsylvania 18503, 1969. 212 pp. $3.95 paper.

The conceptual and procedural framework of this handbook for teachers is described by the authors as that of a humanistic behaviorism incorporating a blend of what is known in education and behavioral science relative to classroom environments. There are two major sections: (1) guidelines for the use of behavior modification procedures in measuring, increasing desirable and decreasing undesirable behaviors, and programming successful learning experiences for children; and (2) guidelines for the use of behavior modification procedures with retarded, socially deprived, deviant, and emotionally disturbed children.

96. McAllister, L. W., Stachowiak, J. G., Baer, D. M., and Conderman, L. The application of operant conditioning techniques in a secondary school classroom. *Journal of Applied Behavior Analysis*, 1969, *2*, 277-285. Available from Dr. Loring W. McAllister, Western Mental Health Center, 438 West Main St., Marshall, Minnesota 56258.

Report on the effects of training a high school teacher to use operant reinforcement procedures to modify two target behaviors: (1) inappropriate talking in class and (2) turning-around, in-seat behavior. The class was a "low-track" junior-senior English class consisting of 25 students, ages sixteen to nineteen with a mean IQ of 94, the majority of whom were from lower socioeconomic backgrounds. The teacher, a 23-year-old female with a B.A. and one year teaching experience, effectively utilized contingent praise and disapproval in successfully reducing the incidence of both target behaviors.

97. McKenzie, H. S., Clark, M., Wolf, M. M., Kothera, R., and Benson, C. Behavior modification of children with learning disabilities using grades as tokens and allowances as back-up reinforcers. *Exceptional Children*, 1968, *34*, 745-752. Available from Dr. Hugh S. McKenzie, Special Education Program, University of Vermont, 2 Colchester Ave., Burlington, Vermont 05401.

Reports on the use of multiple reinforcements for academic progress, e.g., recess, free-time activities, teacher attention, etc. Weekly grades were backed up with allowance payments from parents with ten students, ages ten to thirteen, all of whom were distractable and disruptive, and two or more years below their grade level in one or more subjects. After increases in academic achievement based on multiple reinforcements, further significant increases were made by the use of grades with allowances as back-up reinforcers. See also

McKenzie, H. S. et al. Training consulting teachers to assist elementary teachers in the management and education of handicapped children. *Exceptional Children*, 1970, *37*, 137-143. And McKenzie, H. S. Special education and consulting teachers. Paper presented at the Third Banff International Conference on Behavior Modification, Calgary, Alberta, Canada, 1971. In F. W. Clark, D. R. Evans, and L. A. Hamerlynck (Eds.), *Implementing behavioral programs for schools and clinics.* Research Press Company, Box 3177 Country Fair Station, Champaign, Illinois 61820, 1972. Pp. 103-124 $4.00 paper.

98. McKeown, D. *What to try next with little Rupert: A teacher's manual on behavior modification in the classroom.* 1971, 63 pp. Single copy available from Psychology Department, Georgia Mental Health Institute, 1256 Briarcliff Rd., Atlanta, Georgia 30306.

This manual, based in part on the Ypsilanti Early Education Program Parent Manual on Child Rearing by Wittes and Radin (see 45), was written primarily for classroom teachers for use in inservice training seminars in behavior modification. The author covers the basic steps of defining, identifying, counting, recording, and consequating the behaviors of children. The nature, kinds, means, and guides for the use of reinforcement and positive controls with children—including token systems—are described as well as ignoring undesirable behavior, the use and misuses of punishment, etc. Specific assignments for teachers in learning how to apply behavioral procedures are included along with a variety of helpful forms for carrying out the process. Examples of six children with various problem behaviors are described to illustrate the applicability of behavior modification in teacher-pupil and classroom situations.

99. Mordock, J. B. and Phillips, D. R. The behavior therapist in the schools. *Psychotherapy: Theory, Research and Practice*, 1971, *8*, 231-235. Available from Dr. John B. Mordock, Astor Home for Children, Rhinebeck, New York 12572.

Discussion of procedures carried out in schools by behaviorally-oriented therapists including: (1) individual behavior modification (case of a six-year-old hyperactive boy and thirteen-year-old disruptive girl); (2) teacher training workshops in which teachers learn to use behavioral procedures in their own classrooms; (3) use of contingency management in classrooms; and (4) use of desensitization with particularly anxious or rigid teachers.

100. Morreau, L. E. and Daley, M. F. *Behavioral management in the classroom*. Appleton-Century-Crofts, Educational Division, Meredith Corporation, 440 Park Ave., South, New York, N. Y. 10016, 1972. 149 pp. $4.95 paper.

This is a workbook designed to teach teachers, on a step-by-step basis, how to use and apply principles of behavioral analysis and modification in the classroom setting. The material is presented in a programmed, sequential, understandable manner so that upon completion the teacher is able to carry out the procedures in the management of classroom behavior. Eight major Practicum Exercises are included that enable the teacher: to observe, record, and graph specific, measurable behaviors in students; to differentiate between high and low probability behaviors and to design a contract accordingly; to identify student performance level in an academic skill and accelerate accordingly; to assess and redesign the physical structure of a classroom; to prepare a reinforcement menu for a specific subject; to practice instructing a selected subject using contingency management; and to recapitulate and discuss the results of the previous seven exercises.

101. Nolen, P. A., Kunzelmann, H. P., and Haring, N. G. Behavioral modification in a junior high learning disabilities classroom. *Exceptional Children*, 1967, *34*, 163-168. Available from Dr. Norris G. Haring, Experimental Education Uniṫ, University of Washington, Seattle, Washington 98105.

Study of eight junior high students who were enrolled in a special class on the basis of serious learning disabilities and behavior disorders. Reinforcement contingencies of high value were successfully used to reinforce academic achievement and improved school adjustment in these students.

102. O'Leary, K. D. and O'Leary, S. G. *Classroom management: The successful use of behavior modification*. Pergamon Press, Inc., Maxwell House, Fairview Park, Elmsford, New York 10523, 1972. 664 pp. $5.95 paper.

This book provides a comprehensive, up-to-date coverage of the use of behavioral principles and procedures in classroom and other educational settings. The authors combine their own work and expertise in school applications of behavior modification along with 37 articles most of which report on classroom studies involving the utilization, implementation, and effectiveness of behavioral procedures. Major areas include: behavior modification and psychotherapy with children, use of praise and positive teacher attention, classroom punishment, modeling, token reinforcement systems, peers as reinforcement agents, programmed instruction and teaching machines, the use of para-professionals in educational settings, self-management, and implementing a behavior modification program in the classroom. This book would be a valuable resource in undergraduate and graduate courses in psychology and education, as well as in consultative work and inservice training seminars with teachers and others concerned with the psychological and educational development of children.

103. O'Leary, K. D., Becker, W. C., Evans, M. B., and Saudagras, R. A. A token reinforcement program in a public school: A replication and systematic analysis. *Journal of Applied Behavior Analysis*, 1969, *2*, 3-13. Available from Dr. K. Daniel O'Leary, Department of Psychology, State University of New York, Stony Brook, New York 11790.

Reports on the use of behavior modification procedures with seven members of a second-grade class of 21 children from lower middle class homes who spent over half of their time in various disruptive, unproductive behaviors. Systematic use was made of different conditions including: classroom rules, teacher praise and ignoring, educational structure, a token reinforcement system with back-up reinforcements, etc. The relative effectiveness, generalization, and persistence of these conditions were studied. For a prior, related study, see O'Leary, K. D. and Becker, W. C. Behavior modification of an adjustment class: A token reinforcement program. *Exceptional Children*, 1967, *33*, 637-642. Also for an analysis of the literature on token systems in the management of various behaviors in school settings, see O'Leary, K. D. and Drabman, R. Token reinforcement programs in the classroom: A review. *Psychological Bulletin*, 1971, *75*, 379-398.

104. Patterson, G. R., Cobb, J. A., and Ray, R. S. Direct intervention in the classroom: A set of procedures for the aggressive child. In F. W. Clark, D. R. Evans, and L. A. Hamerlynck (Eds.), *Implementing behavioral programs for schools and clinics*. Research Press, Box 3177 Country Fair Station, Champaign, Illinois 61820, 1972. Pp. 151-201 $4.00 paper.

Report on the use of behavior modification procedures to improve both the social and academic skills of children with various behavioral problems including general disruptiveness, hyperactivity, aggressive, tantrum, destructive behaviors, lying, underachievement, academic failure, etc. The authors describe their "Direct Intervention" approach with 11 boys with a median age of eight-and-one-half years, all from different classrooms and representing some of the more extreme out-of-control problems found in their school and community. This approach involves the mental health consultant demonstrating and modeling the effective use of behavioral procedures directly in the classroom with the teacher observing and, subsequently, being trained to carry out such procedures—shown in the present report to be effective in approximately 90% of consecutive cases with whom they were carried out.

105. Quay, H. C. and Glavin, J. P. *The education of behaviorally disordered children in the public school setting*. Final Report, Project Grant No. 482207, U.S. Office of Education, Bureau of Education of the Handicapped, 1970, 109 pp. mimeographed. Available from Dr. Herbert C. Quay, Division of Educational Psychology, Temple University, Philadelphia, Pennsylvania 19122.

Summary of a four-year project to develop and evaluate procedures for the utilization of behavior modification in the education of behaviorally disordered children in the public schools. Three elementary schools participated: one located in a low socioeconomic area in which all children were black, another located in a low socioeconomic area in which the children were predominantly Caucasian, and the third school was located in a more stable and slightly higher socioeconomic area. The children were in the second through sixth grades; 69 were in the experimental group and 48 in the control group. The majority were hyperactive, disruptive, aggressive, lacking in control, "conduct problems." Token-point systems with a variety of back-up reinforcements including free-time activities, desired objects, resource room, etc., were utilized to accelerate appropriate social behaviors and academic achievements. The authors conclude that the use of behavior modification procedures within the special reinforcement classroom is the most cost-effective method currently available for the education of the behavior problem child in the public school. See also Quay, H. C., Glavin, J. P., and Annesley, F. R., The modification of problem behavior and academic achievement in a resource room. Unpublished paper, 1971.

106. Ramp, E. A. and Hopkins, B. I. (Eds.) *A new direction for education: Behavior analysis 1971, Vol. I.* Department of Human Development, University of Kansas, Lawrence, Kansas 66044, 1971. 369 pp. $3.98 paper.

This volume consists of part of the proceedings of the 1971 University of Kansas Conference on Behavior Analysis in Education, sponsored by the Behavior Analysis Model for Follow Through. There are 19 papers by some 50 contributors, divided into three main sections: (1) Research Reports on Current Topics, e.g., classroom token economies, group contingencies and peer tutoring in academic achievement, self-monitoring in modifying teaching behavior: (2) Current Programs in Behavior Analysis, e.g., training teachers and paraprofessionals in behavior analysis, individualized school adjustment for disturbed children, home-based reinforcements, contracts, and academic behaviors, etc.; and (3) Current Issues, Trends and Directions, guidelines for intervention in school systems. This volume is a collection of some of the most recent and more significant applied contributions of the behavioral model to school, educational, and related settings.

107. Sarason, I. G., Glaser, E. M., and Fargo, G. A. *Reinforcing productive classroom behavior: A teacher's guide to behavior modification.* Behavioral Publications, 2852 Broadway-Morningside Heights, New York, N. Y., 10025, 1972. 43 pp. $3.50 paper.

Originally prepared as one of a series of PREP Reports (Putting Research into Educational Practice) of the National Center for Educational Communications, U. S. Office of Education, this is a practical, nontechnical manual for teachers in learning how to carry out behavior modification procedures to decrease disruptive and increase productive behaviors of pupils in their own classrooms. Various techniques are covered including positive and negative reinforcement, shaping, extinction, token systems, contingency contracts, etc. Examples of applications to children with specific behaviors along with four classroom case studies are included, also a brief glossary and annotated bibliography. Would be useful in inservice work with teachers and others concerned with children.

108. Sattler, H. E. and Swoope, K. S. Token systems: A procedural guide. *Psychology in the Schools*, 1970, *7*, 383-386. Available from Dr. Howard E. Sattler, Department of Educational Psychology, IDP-B Wing, Arizona State University, Tempe, Arizona 85281.

This paper presents guidelines for teachers, school psychologists, and other personnel in applying operant behavior modification principles in the form of token systems in the classroom. Ten steps and procedural considerations are outlined by the authors for the implementation of a classroom token system.

109. Sheppard, W. C., Shank, S. B., and Wilson, D. *How to be a good teacher: Training social behavior in young children.* Research Press, Box 3177 Country Fair Station, Champaign, Illinois 61820, 1972. 93 pp. $3.00 paper.

This manual was written primarily for teachers and other adults who work with preschool-age children in nursery schools, day centers, and other early childhood social environments. It provides a practical, step-by-step guide to the learning and application of behavior modification procedures to nursery school and everyday life experiences of young children. Although written in down-to-earth, easily understandable language, replete with helpful examples and exercises, all of the basic principles and procedures of behavioral psychology necessary in facilitating the healthy development of young children are included. Would be especially useful in training and consultative work with all adult groups who work with young children.

110. Skinner, B. F. *The technology of teaching.* Appleton-Century-Crofts, Educational Division, Meredith Corp., 440 Park Ave., South, New York, N. Y. 10016, 1968. 271 pp. $9.95.

This book contains the major contributions of Professor Skinner relative to the application of operant reinforcement principles and procedures in classroom and other educational settings. Of the eleven chapters that comprise the book, seven have been presented or published previously including: "The Science of Learning and the Art of Teaching," "Teaching Machines," "Motivation of the Student," "The Creative Student," and "Why Teachers Fail." Four chapters were prepared for the present volume: "The Etymology of Teaching," "Discipline, Ethical Behavior, and Self-Control," "A Review of Teaching," and "The Behavior of the Establishment." Although not directly concerned with behavioral deviations and school mental health problems as such, this book would be a valuable reference and resource for consultative work and inservice training for teachers.

111. Skinner, B. F. Contingency management in the classroom. *Education*, 1969, *70*, 93-100. Available from Dr. B. F. Skinner, Department of Psychology, Harvard University, Cambridge, Massachusetts 02138.

Why do students go to school? Behave appropriate or inappropriately in the classroom? Study, learn, and remember? The author answers and discusses these questions in terms of contingencies of reinforcement and the application of behavior modification procedures by teachers in classroom settings. A number of important aspects and considerations relative to operant conditioning in the schools are succinctly discussed including programmed instruction, behavioral objectives, facilitating academic achievement and social skills, the misuse of punishment, token systems, criticisms of operant procedures, suggestions for the training of teachers, etc. This paper would be a valuable reference in inservice training and consultative work with classroom teachers.

112. Staats, A. W., Minke, K. A., and Butts, P. A token-reinforcement remedial reading program administered by black therapy-technicians to problem black children. *Behavior Therapy*, 1970, *1*, 331-353. Available from Dr. Arthur W. Staats, Department of Psychology, University of Hawaii, Honolulu, Hawaii 96822.

Reports on the use of behavior modification procedures carried out by Black nonprofessionals (indigenous workers, high school seniors, and adult volunteers) in remedial reading work with 32 Black, ghetto children with a mean chronological age of about fourteen years and a mean intelligence age of about eight years. All of these children were problem learners along with being emotionally disturbed, antisocial, and/or retarded. This behavioral program, supervised by a classroom teacher with assistance and consultation from a mental health professional, demonstrated the effectiveness of this approach both in terms of improvement in academic progress in children and in the utilization and upgrading of unemployed, Black adults. Additional papers on the use of reinforcement procedures in the acquisition and improvement of reading skills in children are available from Dr. Staats.

113. Stachowiak, J. G. Toward the management of classroom behavior problems: An approach to intervention in a school. Paper prepared for presentation at the First Annual Symposium, Current Issues in Community-Clinical Psychology: School Intervention, University of Maryland, College Park, Maryland, March, 1971. Available from Dr. James G. Stachowiak, Department of Psychology, University of Kansas, Lawrence, Kansas 66044.

Describes a program for providing training and consultation in behavior modification for teachers and other school personnel relative to behavior problems in children. Involves the development of a behavioral intervention approach and evaluation in a county school system utilizing graduate trainee students in clinical psychology at the University of Kansas as consultants.

114. Stephens, T. M. School psychologists as teacher consultants using a behavioral model. Paper presented at the Annual Meeting of the American Psychological Association, Miami Beach, Florida, 1970. Available from Dr. Thomas M. Stephens, Department of Psychology, Ohio State University, Columbus, Ohio 43210.

An outline for consultation to teachers is proposed: (1) assessment, (2) specifying objectives, (3) planning modification strategies, (4) treatment, (5) evaluation. The case of a boy with multiple deviant behaviors illustrates the consultative process.

115. Stern, J. (Ed.) Report of the HEW work group on behavior analysis in education. Unpublished report, 1971, 59 pp. plus four appendices. Information concerning this report may be obtained from Director, Research and Development Planning, Office of the Secretary, Department of Health, Education, and Welfare, Washington, D. C. 20201.

This is a comprehensive report on the present status of behavior modification in school and other educational settings. Major centers of activity involving the use of behavioral procedures are surveyed including: The Learning Village (Ulrich); Project Follow Through (Becker, Bushell); Programming Interpersonal Curricula for Adolescents (Cohen); Teacher Training (Madsen); Responsive Teaching Model (Hall). In addition there are extended discussions of the development of the behavioral model, evaluation of the behavioral model in the classroom, controversial issues, and recommendations for future utilizations in educational work. The appendices include a basic bibliography, selected materials for instructing parents and teachers, applications of behavior analysis, and a list of centers of activity in behavior modification.

116. Stuart, R. B. Behavior modification techniques for the educational technologist. In R. Sarri (Ed.) *Conference Proceedings of the National Workshop on School Social Work, 1969-1970.* National Association of Social Workers, 2 Park Ave., New York, N. Y. 10016. 1972, in press.

Although addressed primarily to school social workers, this material is relevant to all personnel concerned with child and school mental health. Applications of behavioral procedures in schools are discussed including: contingent reinforcement in social control and academic work, varied intervention alternatives available to teachers, reinforcement menus, token systems, use of grades, etc. Advantages of and resistances to the use of the behavioral model in school situations are reviewed. The author suggests school social workers be trained as "educational technologists" to help teachers develop effective behavioral management-teaching-learning environmental systems for children.

117. Sulzer, B. and Mayer, G. R. *Behavior modification procedures for school personnel*. Dryden Press, 2121 Touhy Ave., Elk Grove, Illinois 60004, 1972. 316 pp. $4.95 paper.

Written primarily as a text for courses for professional personnel in elementary and secondary education including teachers, administrators, child, school, and educational psychologists, social workers, counselors, etc., this book presents a comprehensive coverage of the application of operant reinforcement principles to the modification of child behaviors in the classroom and other school settings. Major sections deal with basic procedures in behavior modification, increasing desirable behaviors, teaching new behaviors, maintaining existing behaviors, reducing or eliminating undesirable behaviors, implementing and evaluating school behavior modification programs, etc. A variety of techniques are described including token systems, behavior contracts, Premacking, shaping, chaining, fading, intermittent reinforcement and schedules of reinforcement, extinction, time-out, punishment, etc. Numerous exercises are included to facilitate learning and applying the principles and procedures involved in behavior modification. Also included is a ten-page glossary.

118. Surratt, P. R., Ulrich, R., and Hawkins, R. P. An elementary student as a behavioral engineer. *Journal of Applied Behavior Analysis,* 1969, *2*, 85-92. Available from Dr. Paul R. Surratt, Van Buren County Mental Health Services, Box 219, Bangor, Michigan 49013. Also in R. Ulrich, T. Stachnik, and J. Mabry (Eds.), *Control of Human Behavior, Vol. II: From cure to prevention.* Scott, Foresman & Co., Glenview, Illinois 60025, 1970. Pp. 263-271 $5.50 paper, $7.50 hard.

Reports on a study of the behaviors of four first-grade students in a rural public school, all of whom showed unsatisfactory adjustment, e.g., disruptive classroom behaviors, talking out, poor academic performance, daydreaming, etc. The "behavior modifier" in this study was a fifth-grade student in the same school who was trained to use a console that recorded the target behaviors (e.g., classroom work) and gave feedback to each of the four students. A token-type and

Premack Principle system was used to provide reinforcements for desired behaviors. On the basis of generally favorable results, the authors recommend further exploration and extension of this approach to modifying the behavior of several children simultaneously by means of a student "behavioral engineer."

119. Toews, J. M. The counselor as contingency manager. *Personnel and Guidance Journal*, 1969, *48*, 127-133. Available from Dr. Jay M. Toews, Department of Educational Psychology, Teachers College of the University of Nebraska, Lincoln, Nebraska 68508.

Discussion of how school counselors can function as consultants in behavior modification and contingency management for teachers. Reports on a study carried out in a high school summer session in which graduate students enrolled in a counseling practicum served as "contingency managers" to the classroom teachers. Three case examples are described to illustrate the process of classroom contingency management. The author points out the implications of a behavioral technology for school counseling and education.

120. Ulrich, R., and Arnett, M. Teaching the disadvantaged. Prepublication paper, 1970, 23 pp., mimeographed. Available from Dr. Roger Ulrich, Department of Psychology, Western Michigan University, Kalamazoo, Michigan 49001.

Discusses the use of behavior modification to accelerate academic behaviors and decelerate disruptive behaviors. Several studies are briefly reviewed to demonstrate effective applications by teachers in different classroom situations including the use of a fifth-grade student to modify the behaviors of four first-graders and to increase their academic achievements. The authors also discuss the use of programmed instruction methods and a pyramiding system of education, i.e., persons from college professors to kindergarten children should be trained to help others learn and modify their behaviors. For a description of a preschool program based on behavior modification principles for children between two-and-one-half and five years of age, from both poor and affluent homes, see Ulrich, R. L., Louisell, S. E., and Wolfe, M. The learning village: A behavioral approach to early education. *Educational Technology*, 1971, *11*, 32-45.

121. Ulrich, R., Wolfe, M., and Bluhm, M. Operant conditioning in the public schools. *Behavior Modification Monographs, I,* no. 1, 1970. Available from Dr. Roger Ulrich, Department of Psychology, Western Michigan University, Kalamazoo, Michigan 49001. A shortened version has been published in R. Ulrich, T. Stachnik, and J. Mabry (Eds.), *Control of human behavior, Vol. II: From cure to prevention.* Scott, Foresman & Co., Glenview, Illinois 60025, 1970. Pp. 334-343 $5.50 paper, $7.50 hard.

Concerned with how mental health professionals can help teachers function as "experts" in dealing with behavioral problems of elementary school children who would ordinarily be referred to outside agencies for treatment because of disruptive, destructive, and other deviant behaviors. Describes inservice training programs for teachers in learning how to use behavior modification techniques and discusses the initial resistances and objections of teachers to such techniques. Also describes applications to a preschool group in which children two to four years of age learn basic skills in reading, writing, and arithmetic.

122. Valett, R. E. *Effective teaching: A guide to diagnostic prescriptive task analysis.* Fearon Publishers, 6 Davis Dr., Belmont, California 94002, 1970. 82 pp. $3.25 paper.

Written as a guide for classroom teachers, with particular reference to children with various learning disabilities. The essence of "diagnostic-prescriptive task analysis" involves a description of learning problems and teaching objectives in behavioral terms and a structuring of the teacher-pupil learning situation, including sequential interactions, step-by-step work toward specific learning outcomes with systematic reinforcement, and a daily recording of the child's progress—all of this being based on a behavioral profile of each child. A number of behavior modification procedures are described including a variety of contingency systems, token techniques, learning contracts, negative reinforcement, punishment, etc. This material would be suitable for inservice training programs for teachers and special education teachers. For a previous discussion of a token reinforcement system to increase positive and decrease negative behaviors in children in classroom situations, see also Valett, R. E. A social reinforcement technique for the classroom management of behavior disorders. *Exceptional Children*, 1966, *33*, 185-189. Available from Dr. Robert E. Valett, Department of Advanced Studies, Fresno State College, Fresno, California 93706.

123. Ward, M. H., and Baker, B. L. Reinforcement therapy in the classroom. *Journal of Applied Behavior Analysis*, 1968, *1*, 323-328. Available from Dr. Michael H. Ward, Department of Social Relations, William James Hall, Harvard University, Cambridge, Massachusetts 02138.

A study of the effectiveness of reinforcement in the form of systematic use of attention and praise by the teacher in reducing disruptive and inattentive classroom behaviors of four first grade children in an urban public school. Teachers were trained to ignore deviant behaviors and to attend and praise task-appropriate behaviors with emphasis on immediacy, consistency, and contingency in the application of reinforcement procedures. In general, significant decreases in disruptive and increases in relevant behaviors were obtained, leading the authors to conclude that teachers can be trained to function as effective "therapists" in reinforcement techniques in the classroom.

124. Wasik, B. H. The application of Premack's generalization on reinforcement to the management of classroom behavior. *Journal of Experimental Child Psychology*, 1970, *10*, 33-43. Available from Dr. Barbara H. Wasik, School of Education, University of North Carolina, Chapel Hill, North Carolina 27514.

Reports on the successful use of behavior modification procedures in a second grade class of a demonstration school for culturally deprived children. The focus of the study was on the systematic application of the Premack Principle, i.e., a less probable behavior, e.g., studying in the classroom, can be increased by making a more probable behavior, e.g., recess or free-choice activities in the classroom contingent on the prior occurrence of the less probable behavior. The behavioral procedures were effective with the entire class of twenty children whose Wechsler IQ's ranged from 74 to 130. See also Wasik, B. H., Senn, K., Welch, R. H., and Cooper, B. R. Behavior modification with culturally deprived school children: Two case studies. *Journal of Applied Behavior Analysis*, 1969, *2*, 181-194.

125. Wetzel, R. J. Behavior modification techniques and the training of teacher's aides. *Psychology in the Schools*, 1970, *7*, 325-330. Available from Dr. Ralph J. Wetzel, Department of Psychology, University of Arizona, Tucson, Arizona 85721.

A four-week training program in behavior modification for teaching personnel of two federally-supported child day care centers is described. Five trainee groups, each with a teacher and two or more aides from poverty area populations, participated. Seven of the teachers were Black, five Mexican-American, and two Anglo. Emphasis was on how to observe and specify behavior, modeling of procedures by the staff, providing corrective feedback, and especially on the identification and reinforcement of appropriate behaviors. Evaluation of the effectiveness of the training program was in terms of video tapes, behavioral measures and task structured situations, and attitude measures.

126. Whelan, R. J. and Haring, N. G. Modification and maintenance of behavior through systematic application of consequences. *Exceptional Children*, 1966, *32*, 281-289. Available from Dr. Richard J. Whelan, Special Education, Children's Rehabilitation Unit, University of Kansas Medical Center, Kansas City, Kansas 66103.

A general discussion of the use of behavior modification procedures by teachers of children with various behavioral deviations and learning disabilities. Examples, advantages, and problems in the application of operant behavioral principles in special education settings are discussed.

127. Wolf, M. M., Giles, D. K., and Hall, R. V. Experiments with token reinforcement in a remedial classroom. *Behaviour Research and Therapy*, 1968, *6*, 51-64. Available from Dr. Montrose M. Wolf, Department of Human Development, University of Kansas, Lawrence, Kansas 66044.

Reports on results of the first year of an after-school remedial education project for 16 low-achieving fifth and sixth grade children from an urban poverty area who were two or more years below their grade level in reading. These pupils attended a remedial classroom each week day afternoon and on Saturday morning for two and one-half hours. A token-point system for appropriate behaviors and academic achievement involving various redeemable reinforcements (e.g., snacks, candies, novelties, going to the zoo, circus, swimming, etc.) was used throughout the project which was carried out by a head teacher, two teaching assistants, and two Neighborhood Youth Corps employees. Evaluation of the effectiveness of this project was based on comparisons with a control group who had no remedial program and demonstrated significantly greater gains in academic achievement for the remedial-reinforcement group.

Applications with Parents and Teachers

3

128. Bijou, S. W. and Baer, D. M. (Eds.) *Child development: Readings in experimental analysis.* Appleton-Century-Crofts, 440 Park Ave. South, New York, New York 10016, 1967. 408 pp. $4.50 paper.

A collection of twenty-five readings by the editors and a number of other outstanding contributors concerned with the applied experimental analysis and modification of child behavior in what is referred to as the natural science approach to child development and behavior problems in children. The operant framework of this book is divided into three major sections: (1) basic behavioral principles; (2) applications to social behaviors, deviant behaviors, rehabilitation, and to home and educational settings; (3) review and overview of the field.

129. Blackham, G. J. and Silberman, A. *Modification of child behavior.* Wadsworth Publishing Co., Inc., Belmont, California 94002, 1971. 186 pp. $3.95 paper.

Specifically written for workers in mental health and education concerned with facilitating normal and decreasing deviant behaviors in children. Based on a substantial coverage of the recent literature on applied work and research, the emphasis is on the use of behavior modification procedures in the home, in the classroom, and in the mental health clinic or special education setting. A variety of behavior problems in children, with which parents and teachers can be trained to cope, are discussed along with step-by-step outlines for carrying out the behavior change process by means of extinction, positive reinforcement, modeling, role shifting, time-out, withdrawal from reinforcement, behavioral contracts, etc. This book would be useful in work with parents, teachers, and others concerned with children.

130. Bradfield, R. H. (Ed.) *Behavior modification of learning disabilities.* Academic Therapy Publications, 1539 Fourth St., San Rafael California 94901, 1971. 172 pp. $3.95 paper.

This book consists of twelve selections, half of which were previously published and the other half which were written for this volume; the contents are divided into three sections: (1) General Applications of Behavior Modification in Educational and Social Environments; (2) Behavior Modification and the Remediations of Learning Disabilities; and (3) Specific Behavior Modification Program Models in Classroom Situations. The focus of this book is on how parents and teachers can be helped to carry out therapeutic education with their own children—particularly those with learning disabilities, social deficits, and other developmental handicaps. Major topics covered include: behavioral analysis of learning disabilities, therapeutic reeducation of delinquent youth, precision teaching in special education, training parents in the management of children with deviant behaviors, remedial education in reading and language and increasing attention span, demonstrations of the effective use of behavior modification procedures in elementary and junior high school classrooms for students with learning disabilities.

131. Brown, D. G. Behavior modification with children. *Mental Hygiene*, 1972, *56*, 22-30. Available from the Phoenix Area Indian Health Service, Mental Health Branch, 1440 East Indian School Rd., Phoenix, Arizona 85014.

Brief overview of developments in behavior modification in relation to children and youth including: basic concepts and procedures, advantages, application to various deviant behaviors, criticisms and resistances to behavior modification, and mental health manpower implications.

132. Cantrell, R. P., Cantrell, M. L., Huddleston, C. M., and Wooldridge, R. L. Contingency contracting with school problems. *Journal of Applied Behavior Analysis*, 1969, *2*, 215-220. Available from Dr. Robert P. Cantrell, Child and Youth Development Center, Tennessee Department of Mental Health, 3420 Richards St., Nashville, Tennessee 37215.

Reports on the use of written Contigency Contracts prepared by mental health professionals for use by parents and/or teachers in decreasing various problem behaviors (e.g., truancy, disruptive, aggressive behaviors, stealing, low academic achievement, etc.) and increasing appropriate behaviors in their children enrolled in public schools, first through eleventh grades. Individual Point System Contracts were based on the behavioral analysis of each child's problem(s) and preferred reinforcements, and indicated the kinds of tasks and activities together with their worth in points for each individual child who could earn up to 50 points per day or 250 points per week; the points, in turn, could be exchanged for the preferred reinforcement, e.g., going places, watching TV, spending money, etc. The child's teacher marked points earned at school and his parents those earned at home. Separate record sheets were maintained for points earned and points spent. Overall results were favorable and suggested further development of the contingency contracting approach.

133, Champagne, D. W. and Goldman, R. M. *Teaching parents teaching.* Appleton-Century-Crofts, Educational Division, Meredith Corp., 440 Park Ave. South, New York, N. Y. 10016, 1972. 268 pp. $5.95 paper.

A programmed text based on reinforcement, behavior modification principles and designed to help teachers become effective teachers of parents. The rationale is based on the importance of parents and teachers supplementing each other in helping children learn; and the overall goal is to help teachers to help parents carry out a consistent, positive reinforcement pattern of interaction with their children including the reinforcement of skills that are taught in the school. This book provides a parent-training program for teachers to carry out—complete with step-by-step applications—training strategies, exercises, etc. It covers both preschool and primary as well as upper elementary and high school grades and includes descriptions of nine parents who completed the training program presented by the authors.

134. Cohen, S. I., Keyworth, J. M., Kleiner, R. I., and Libert, J. M. *The support of school behaviors by home-based reinforcement via parent-child contingency contracts.* Behavior Service Consultants, Box 186, Greenbelt, Maryland 20770, 1971. 21 pp. plus appendices. $3.00 paper. Related materials available from Dr. Shlomo I. Cohen at the same address.

This material, based on a presentation at the Second Kansas Symposium on Behavior Analysis in Education, May, 1971, describes the overall program and, in particular, the parent consultation program at the Anne Arundel Learning Center in Maryland. This center is a public school for approximately 150 students, twelve to seventeen years of age, who were unable to remain in regular schools because of academic and/or social deficits; most of these students had prior contacts with mental health agencies as well as juvenile courts. A token system with appropriate back-up reinforcements is used for both academic achievement and desirable social behaviors. The parent training program is designed to help parents carry out behavior modification procedures with their own children, using effective home-based reinforcements. Extensive use is made of contingency contracts involving the child and his parents. The authors discuss the nature and advantages of behavior contracts, describe the use of such contracts with two teenagers and their parents, and include seven examples of actual contracts used in the parent training program.

135. Copeland, R. E. Juniper Gardens children's intervention treatment programs in home, school, and community. Paper prepared for presentation at the Nashville Showcase of Innovative Treatment Programs in Child Mental Health, Nashville, Tennessee, 1972. Available from Dr. Rodney E. Copeland, Juniper Gardens Children's Project, 2021 North Third, Kansas City, Kansas 66101.

The author reviews and summarizes the use of behavior modification procedures as the major intervention approach to various groups of disadvantaged children and youth in the Kansas City, Kansas, area including work with parents and families, teachers, school, and other community programs.

136. Deibert, A. N. and Harmon, A. J. *New tools for changing behavior.* Research Press, Box 3177 Country Fair Station, Champaign, Illinois 61820, 1970. 135 pp. $4.00 paper.

This semi-programmed, self-instructional manual was written for persons who, though not formally trained in mental health, are interested in understanding and applying basic behavior modification principles in improving their relations with others and their adjustment in everyday life. Although concerned with human beings generally, the emphasis is on children and adolescents in terms of the use of behavior modification procedures by parents, teachers, and others to facilitate normal and eliminate deviant behaviors. Includes descriptions of a number of children with various problem behaviors to illustrate the applications of operant reinforcement techniques. This manual would be helpful in consultative work with parents and inservice training with teachers.

137. *Educational Technology,* 1971*, 11.* Educational Technology Publications, Inc., 140 Sylvan Ave., Englewood Cliffs, New Jersey 07632 $3.95 (February issue).

This special issue consists of 14 papers all concerned with recent developments in preschool education. Six of these papers focus on the use of behavior modification procedures by parents and teachers with preschool children: (1) teaching child-rearing skills to parents; (2) a behavioral approach to learning in preschool children, ages two to thirty months; (3) an operant reinforcement approach to preschool child rearing and education; (4) behavioral intervention with a variety of handicapped children in preschool settings; (5) a brief review of research in behavior modification in the home and school; and (6) a brief review of applications of learning principles to reading in preschool children.

138. Eron, L. D., Walder, L. O., and Lefkowitz, M. M. *Learning of aggression in children.* Little, Brown and Co., 34 Beacon St., Boston, Massachusetts 02106, 1971. 311 pp. $9.95.

This book is based on research findings of a survey of aggression in school settings in several hundred third grade, eight-year-old boys and girls in Columbia County, New York. The authors use a learning and sociobehavioral conceptual framework in discussing their work. Four major variables are studied as important antecedents in the determination of aggressive behavior in children: (1) instigation or the extent of frustrating conditions such as parental rejection, chronic criticism, disharmony, lack of nurturance; (2) identification and role modeling of aggression by parents and others; (3) reinforcement of aggressive behavior; and (4) sociocultural factors such as economic and educational levels, ethnicity, gender, etc. Separate chapters are devoted to each of these variables. Chapter 9, "Implications for Child-Rearing," is specifically concerned with the application of learning and behavior modification principles in the management of aggression in children by parents and teachers. Four examples of behavior modification involving either too much or too little aggression in children are discussed. An appendix, "Operant Conditioning of Aggression" is also included to help parents and teachers "learn how to do it."

139. Ferster, C. B. and Simons, J. Behavior therapy with children. *Psychological Record*, 1966, *16*, 65-71. Available from Dr. Charles B. Ferster, Department of Psychology, American University, Washington, D. C. 20016.

Discussion of the use, relevance, and importance of reinforcements that are present and occur in the natural environments of children. This is in contrast to the usual operant paradigm that follows the model of food reinforcement procedures used in developing or modifying animal behavior. Natural reinforcers for children are those conditions or activities in the lives of children which, when used as contingencies, can help develop, strengthen, or weaken particular behavior in children. Several children in a Day Treatment Center are described in relation to the teacher's utilization of naturally occurring events to modify designated behaviors of handicapped children. The authors stress the necessity of helping parents learn how to use contingencies of reinforcement in the home in order to maintain behavioral improvements achieved in the clinic or school.

140. Graziano, A. M. A group treatment approach to multiple problem behaviors of autistic children. *Exceptional Children*, 1970, *36*, 765-770. Available from Dr. Anthony M. Graziano, Department of Psychology, State University of New York, Buffalo, New York 14214.

Describes a day care program extending over a period of about four years for four severely autistic children, plus several others added later to the original group. These children, ages five to nine, showed markedly bizarre and disturbed behaviors (unresponsiveness, little or no speech, social aloofness and indifference to people, unpredictable and violent outbursts, destructiveness, etc.). With training and supervision by a mental health professional, teacher-aide type high school level mental health workers were able to carry out this project and function as "therapists" for these severely disturbed children. Results of this project demonstrated that significant and enduring improvement can be accomplished with such children in self care, social behavior, language development, academic skills, etc. Parents of these children were helped to carry out similar behavior modification techniques in the home. The author emphasizes the importance of training parents for parallel home applications of reinforcement contingencies.

141. Gregersen, G. F. Behavior modification training for parents and teachers. Materials available from Dr. Gayle F. Gregersen, Director, Behavior Modification Training Center, 27 "C" St., Salt Lake City, Utah 84103.

Describes training programs in behavior modification for parents, teachers, and others concerned with children in connection with a psychoeducational day treatment center for children, ages three to twelve, with various behavior problems, learning or developmental disorders, educational retardation, etc. For a report of a parent and teacher training project involving mental health professionals, teachers, graduate students, aides, and grandparent assistants, see Gregersen, G. F., Sloane, H., Latham, G., and Murdock, E. A classroom approach to multiple behavior and academic problems in retarded and disturbed children. Paper presented at the Annual Meeting of the National Society for Programmed Instruction, San Antonio, Texas, 1968. See also, Gregersen, G. F. Community behavior modification training center for disturbed, autistic and retarded children. Paper prepared for presentation at the Nashville Showcase of Innovative Treatment Programs in Child Mental Health, Nashville, Tennessee, 1972.

142. Guerney, B. G., Jr., (Ed.) *Psychotherapeutic agents: New roles for nonprofessionals, parents, and teachers.* Holt, Rinehart and Winston, Inc., 383 Madison Ave., New York, New York 10017, 1969. 595 pp. $10.50.

This is a book of 48 readings, the focus of which is on ways of meeting the mental health needs of people, particularly children and youth. The contents would be of interest not only to mental health professionals but to teachers, special education personnel, counselors, and administrators in mental health, educational, and other programs concerned with the psychological well-being and social welfare of children and youth. While the concern is with the whole problem of

54

mental health manpower and utilization with reference to all kinds of new personnel, there are three major sections of direct relevance to the present bibliography; these sections include a number of read ings on the use of: (1) peers, (2) parents, and (3) teachers as therapeutic agents for emotionally disturbed, deviant, and other handicapped children. Fifteen of the readings are specifically concerned with the application of behavior modification principles by parents, teachers, and other significant individuals in the lives of children. The readings in these areas include some of the more important contributtions in the field today.

143. Hall, R. V. *Managing behavior.* Part I, *Behavior modification—The measurement of behavior;* Part II, *Behavior modification—Basic principles;* Part III, *Behavior modification—Applications in school and home.* H & H Enterprises, Inc., Box 3342, Lawrence, Kansas 66044, 1970. Each Part, $1.55; Series, $4.65 paper.

This is a series of three booklets concerned specifically with helping parents and teachers to learn how to use behavior modification in the management of their own children and pupils. Basic principles, procedures, step-by-step applications, and case examples in the home and in the school are presented. These booklets are based on the author's extensive work with parents and teachers in helping them cope with various behavior problems and to apply behavioral principles to facilitate the normal development of children. This material would be suitable and helpful in mental health counseling or consultative work with parents and teachers. Information on additional materials in this series available from Dr. R. Vance Hall, 2021 North Third, Kansas City, Kansas 66101.

144. Hall, R. V., Cristler, C., Cranston, S. S., and Tucker, B. Teachers and parents as researchers using multiple baseline designs. *Journal of Applied Behavior Analysis*, 1970, *3*, 247-255. Available from Dr. R. Vance Hall, Bureau of Child Research, Juniper Gardens Children's Project, 2021 North Third, Kansas City, Kansas 66101.

Report on two teachers and parents who used three multiple baseline designs (i.e., identifying and recording several behaviors over time so that several baselines are established) in carrying out behavior modification procedures in the classroom and at home. Target behaviors included: tardiness in a fifth grade class, daily French quiz grades of three high school students, and home activities of a ten-year-old girl involving clarinet practice, Campfire project work, and reading. Results showed marked increases in desired behaviors and demonstrate the feasibility of training parents and teachers in the use of operant reinforcement and contingency management procedures with their own children and pupils.

145. Haring, N. G., Hayden, A. H., and Nolen, P. A. Accelerating appropriate behavior of children in a Head Start program. *Exceptional Children,* 1969, *35,* 773-784. Available from Dr. Norris G. Haring, Experimental Education Unit, Child Development and Retardation Center, University of Washington, Seattle, Washington 98105.

A training and demonstration project involving a classroom of 12 children with severe emotional, social, and/or language deficits, in which Head Start teachers were successfully trained to use behavior modification procedures in decreasing deviant and increasing productive behaviors.

146. Hawkins, R. P., Sluyter, D. J., and Smith, C. D. Modification of achievement by a simple technique involving parents and teacher. In M. B. Harris (Ed.), *Classroom uses of behavior modification.* Charles E. Merrill, 1300 Alum Creek Dr., Columbus, Ohio 43216, 1972. Pp. 101-119 $4.95 paper.

Concerned with the question, What can parents and teachers do to help underachieving children who are neither seriously disturbed nor economically deprived? A single-subject design was used with seven elementary age school children, six of whom showed significant improvements with regard to the target behaviors, e.g., lack of interest in school work, low achievement in arithmetic, reading, spelling, social studies, etc. The school-home procedure involved the teacher giving each child dittoed notes each day regarding the child's performance with respect to the designated subject for improvement; these notes were taken home and appropriate back-up reinforcements provided by the parents. Four of the cases are discussed in detail to illustrate the technique and various effects produced. The authors conclude that school counselors, social workers, psychologists, principals, as well as teachers and parents, can initiate similar reinforcement systems to increase academic progress in low-achieving students. See also Sluyter, D. J. and Hawkins, R. P. Delayed reinforcement of classroom behavior by parents, *Journal of Learning Disabilities,* 1972, *5,* 20-28. Available from Dr. Robert P. Hawkins, Department of Psychology, Western Michigan University, Kalamazoo, Michigan 49001.

147. Kroth, R. L., Whelan, R. J., and Stables, J. M. Teacher application of behavior principles in home and classroom environments. *Focus on Exceptional Children,* 1970, *1,* 1-12. Available from Dr. Roger Kroth, Special Education, Children's Rehabilitation Unit, University of Kansas Medical Center, Kansas City, Kansas 66103.

A discussion of the training of parents and teachers in the use of behavior modification procedures both in the classroom and in the home with children having academic and nonacademic behavior problems. Also reports on a study involving the parents and teachers of five junior high school students who had been psychiatrically diagnosed as "emotionally disturbed." A series of parent-teacher training conferences were held with focus on applications of behavioral principles by parents within the home which brought about significantly positive changes in both the home and school adjustment of these children. The authors suggest that the development of the behavior modification model has made it possible for parents and teachers to become active and collaborative participants in assisting children to change their behaviors in terms of productive and more satisfying dimensions.

148. Kurtz, D. and Palumbo, A. *The ABC's of child management. Workbooks 1, 2, 3, and 4.* Infomatics, Department A, 8531 Schaefer Highway, Detroit, Michigan 48228, 1971. Each workbook, $1.50.

Each workbook in this series is concerned with the practical applications of behavior modification with children as follows: *Workbook 1* is concerned with basic procedures in the use of reinforcement principles, e.g., specifying behavior, the role of environmental consequences on behavior, how to talk to children, parental discipline, etc.; *Workbook 2* is concerned with the use of reinforcement procedures (the What, Why, Kinds, and Hows of Rewards) by teachers in regular and special education classes to increase students' academic and social behaviors; *Workbook 3* is concerned with teaching parents and teachers how to use time-out procedures to decrease undesirable behavior in children; and *Workbook 4*, which is based on and extends the contents of *Workbooks 1, 2,* and *3,* is concerned with helping parents, teachers, and other professionals function more effectively as trainers and teachers in the field of child management. All of these workbooks are self-instructional in format and are replete with familiar examples and everyday applications that facilitate learning the fundamentals of behavior modification. In addition, four 25-minute films have been produced, each one to be used in conjunction with each respective workbook. (See film section, 233, for description of each of these films.)

149. Larsen, L. A. and Bricker, W. A. *A manual for parents and teachers of severely and moderately retarded children.* Institute on Mental Retardation and Intellectual Development, John F. Kennedy Center for Research on Education and Human Development, Peabody College for Teachers, Nashville, Tennessee 37203, Vol. V, No. 22, 1968. 138 pp. $1.00 paper.

This manual was written specifically for parents, teachers, and others who work with retarded children, to provide a basis for understanding and applying principles of behavior modification. The material is clearly presented in a practical way that facilitates direct applications. Specific activities are covered such as toilet training, putting on clothes, eating correctly, language acquisition, etc. Although designed for work with the retarded, parents and teachers concerned with young children of any mental level would find this manual helpful.

150. Lindsley, O. R. Training parents and teachers to precisely manage children's behavior. Paper presented at the C. S. Mott Foundation Children's Health Center, Flint, Michigan, 1968. Available from the Charles Stewart Mott Foundation, Program Administration, 510 Mott Foundation Building, Flint, Michigan 48502.

The author discusses his four-step procedure of Pinpointing, Recording, Consequating, and Trying Again in behavior modification work. These steps are clearly described, explained, and illustrated with a number of examples of children with a variety of deviant behaviors both in the home and in the school. This approach developed by Lindsley has been used with favorable results by a number of other workers in child and school mental health. This material would be helpful for mental health personnel who work with and offer training courses for parents and teachers to help them learn how to carry out behavior modification procedures with their own children and pupils. For an earlier discussion of related interest, see Lindsley, O. R. Theoretical basis of behavior modification. Paper presented at the School of Education, University of Oregon, Eugene, Oregon, 1967. Available from Dr. Ogden R. Lindsley, Bureau of Child Research, University of Kansas, 9 Bailey Hall, Lawrence, Kansas 66044.

151. Martin, D. H. Teaching child management techniques to parents: A new approach. Paper presented at the Annual Meeting of the American Association of Psychiatric Services for Children, Beverly Hills, California, 1971. Available from Dr. Daun H. Martin, Huntsville-Madison County Mental Health Center, 218 Randolph Ave., Huntsville, Alabama 35801.

The author reports on the development and implementation of training courses in child management for parents offered as a community service of the Huntsville Mental Health Center. The purpose of the initial course was to help parents learn how to decrease deviant behaviors and how to facilitate desirable behaviors through the use of behavior modification with their own children. The second course was offered to parents as well as social workers, teachers, and nurses and met for five weekly two-hour sessions. Following the third course, which consisted of both parents and professional personnel, 11 separate courses were offered either for parents or for professionals in mental health, education, medicine, nursing, social work, rehabilitation counseling, etc. The author discusses the goals, results, and effectiveness of the 14 separate courses in child management. Demonstrates the contribution a mental health center can make through consultation, education, and training for parents and others concerned with children. See also Martin, D. H. Program in child and youth treatment and management for parents and community groups. Paper prepared for presentation at the Nashville Showcase on Innovative Treatment Programs in Child Mental Health, Nashville, Tennessee, 1972

152. Mira, M. Results of a behavior modification training program for parents and teachers. *Behaviour Research and Therapy*, 1970, *8*, 309-311. Available from Dr. Mary Mira, Children's Rehabilitation Unit, University of Kansas Medical Center, Kansas City, Kansas 66103.

Summarizes results of a behavior modification training program for parents and occasionally teachers in learning how to manage behavior problems in their own children and pupils. This program, which was carried out by mental health professionals and doctoral students at the University of Kansas, Children's Rehabilitation Unit, covered a 21-month period and involved 113 children, ages eighteen months to sixteen years, with various behavior problems and other handicaps.

153. Patterson, G. R. A community mental health program for children. In L. A. Hamerlynck, P. O. Davidson, and L. E. Acker (Eds.), *Behavior modification and ideal mental health services*. University of Calgary, Calgary, Alberta, Canada, 1969. Pp. 130-179 $3.00 paper.

In connection with a research proposal to develop comprehensive community mental health intervention and preventive services for children, the author provides an extended summary and discussion of the literature relative to the use of behavior modification both in the school and in the home including the training of teachers and parents as primary "intervention agents" for their own pupils and children.

154. Patterson, G. R. and Gullion, M. E. *Living with children: New methods for parents and teachers.* Research Press, Box 3177 Country Fair Station, Champaign, Illinois 61820, 1971. 125 pp. $3.00 paper.

Written as a practical guide and programmed manual concerned with helping parents and teachers understand and learn how to modify various behaviors of children. Specific chapters outline the use of operant behavior modification with children who are: (1) overly aggressive, (2) overly negativistic, (3) hyperactive, (4) overdependent, (5) fearful, and (6) withdrawn. Based on extensive applied research with families. Would be helpful as assigned reading material in training and consultative work with parents and/or teachers. For a discussion of the successful use of behavior modification procedures by parents, teachers, and peer group in reprogramming the social environment of a five-year-old boy with multiple deviant, aggressive, and destructive behaviors, see Patterson, G. R. and Brodsky, G. A. Behaviour modification programme for a child with multiple problem behaviours. *Journal of Child Psychology and Psychiatry,* 1966, *7*, 277-295. Available from Dr. Gerald R. Patterson, Oregon Research Institute, 488 East 11th Ave., Eugene, Oregon 97403.

155. Ray, R. S. Parents and teachers as therapeutic agents in behavior modification. Paper presented at the Second Annual Alabama Behavior

Modification Institute, Tuscaloosa, Alabama, 1969. Available from Dr. Roberta S. Ray, Oregon Research Institute, 488 East 11th Ave., Eugene, Oregon 97403.

Summarizes extensive work both with parents in the home and with teachers in school involving the application of behavior modification intervention procedures with boys between the ages of six and fourteen, all of whom had been described as "severe conduct disorders." These multiple behavior problems included: academic failures, hyperactivity, social isolation, extreme aggressiveness, stealing, vandalism, firesetting. See also Ray, R. S., and Shaw, D. A., and Cobb, J. A. The work box: An innovation in teaching attentional behavior. *School Counselor*, 1970, *18*, 15-35, for further discussion of behavioral procedures in classroom situations. Also, Ray, R. S. Direct intervention and reprogramming the social environments of disturbed and delinquent children and youth. Paper prepared for presentation at the Nashville Showcase of Innovative Treatment Programs in Child Mental Health, Nashville, Tennessee, 1972.

156. Ross, A. O. The application of behavior principles in therapeutic education. *Journal of Special Education*, 1967, *1*, 275-286. Available from Dr. Alan O. Ross, Department of Psychology, State University of New York, Stony Brook, New York 11790.

The essentials of operant reinforcement are discussed in terms of applications to children by parents and particularly by teachers. The author contrasts the traditional psychodynamic clinical approach with the conceptualization and procedures of behavior modification relative to emotionally disturbed and other handicapped children; he also discusses various objections and resistances to behavior modification. Several studies are briefly reviewed to illustrate the relevance and applicability of this approach by parents and teachers, and the author concludes that mental health workers can help these groups function as therapeutic educators.

157. Shields, J. A. Training parents and teachers in the application of behavior modification principles. In *Harford-Cecil supplementary education center: A handbook of activities, 1970-1971.* Available from Dr. Joseph A. Shields, 851 Revolution St., Havre de Grace, Maryland 21078.

A brief description of successful training classes for parents and elementary school teachers in the use of operant reinforcement procedures with children. Also describes the use of behavior modification in a rehabilitation class of adolescent boys with delinquent and/or other deviant behaviors.

158. Stover, D. O. Home and community treatment. *Newsletter: Wisconsin Psychiatric Institute,* 1970, no. 2, 11-13. Available from Dr.

60

Donald O. Stover, Wisconsin Children's Treatment Center, 3418 Harper Rd., Madison, Wisconsin 53704.

Describes the development of an intensive treatment program based on the behavior modification model for severely disturbed children in their own homes, schools, and communities. As an alternative to hospitalizing or placing the child in an institution, mental health staff members of the Children's Center including trained child-care workers carry out the behavioral treatment process by working directly with the child and his family in their home and with the child, his teachers, and peers in the school. During the first week, the staff make extended observational visits to the child's home and school in order to identify the kinds, frequency, and circumstances of deviant behaviors in the parent-child or teacher-child interactions, etc. Child-care workers, trained in the application of behavior modification procedures, provide demonstrations, training, and ongoing assistance to the primary adults in the child's life, i.e., parents, teachers, relatives, neighbors, etc. The author reports on the first nine months of this demonstration project involving 13 families with severely disturbed children. The majority required several hours of child care per day during the initial weeks of treatment. Although three of the children had to be removed from their homes, the author's conclusion is favorable as to the feasibility, effectiveness, and economy (cost may be one-half to one-third less than hospitalization) of the home and community treatment approach.

159. *Teaching Exceptional Children*, Spring, 1971, *3*. The Council for Exceptional Children, Jefferson Plaza, Suite 900, Arlington, Virginia 22202. $1.50 (Spring Issue).

This entire issue is on precision teaching and the behavioral management of children. Discussions include: "Precision Teaching in Perspective: An Interview with Ogden R. Lindsley," "Parent Classes In Precise Behavior Management," "Peers and Precision," and "Applying Precision Teaching to Academic Assessment." The material in this issue would be helpful in working both with teachers and parents in terms of using behavioral procedures in increasing positive and decreasing inappropriate behaviors in children.

160. Tramontana, J. A review of research on behavior modification in the home and school. *Educational Technology*, 1971, *11*, 61-64. Available from Dr. Joseph Tramontana, Regional Mental Health and Retardation Center, Anchorage Building, Oxford, Mississippi 38655.

A brief review of some of the problems and discussion of the importance of carrying out behavioral changes in children in natural, everyday, environmental settings. This paper is based on the author's unpublished extensive review of the literature, Behavior modification in the home and in the school: Methods of measuring effectiveness, 1969.

161. Valett, R. E. *Modifying children's behavior: A guide for parents and professionals.* Fearon Publishers, 6 Davis Dr., Belmont, California 94002, 1969. 66 pp. $2.75 paper.

This manual was written as an aid to help parents deal with their children's problems. A variety of problems are presented together with possible solutions and applications of behavioral principles. The material can be used by parents for their own instruction, with individual parent counseling, with parent education groups, and with in-service training for teachers. Includes a number of techniques, aids, etc., that can be utilized and applied by parents, teachers, and others

162. Wahler, R. G. Setting generality: Some specific and general effects of child behavior therapy. *Journal of Applied Behavior Analysis,* 1969, *2,* 239-246. Available from Dr. Robert G. Wahler, Department of Psychology, University of Tennessee, Knoxville, Tennessee 37916.

This study involved two boys, ages five and eight years, who had been referred by teachers to an outpatient clinic for various disruptive behaviors and psychological problems both at school and in the home. Mental health personnel worked with the parents to help them modify undesirable behaviors in their sons through the use of reinforcement contingencies in the home. The major concern of the study was whether changes in school behaviors would also occur as a result of changes in the home. Results showed considerable improvement in desired behaviors in the home but no corresponding change in the classroom. The author discusses the implications of these findings for behavior modification work with children.

163. Wahler, R. G. and Erickson, M. Child behavior therapy: A community program in Appalachia. *Behaviour Research and Therapy,* 1969, *7,* 71-78. Available from Dr. Robert G. Wahler, Department of Psychology, University of Tennessee, Knoxville, Tennessee 37916.

Describes a community program based on reinforcement therapy involving the use of volunteer workers (e.g., teachers, counselors, public health nurse) as child behavior therapists in home and school settings. This program was developed in a psychological clinic of a county health center located in Appalachia where there was widespread poverty, unemployment, welfare need, and a low education level; 95% of the referrals to the clinic were children. Effectiveness of the program over a two-year period is discussed and shows that with adequate consultation from mental health professionals, volunteer groups and other community personnel can learn to use behavior modification in working with various behavior problems in children.

164. Watson, L. S., Jr. *Franklin county children's behavior modification program, 1971 project report.* Material available from Dr. Luke S.

Watson, Jr., Director, Columbus State Institute Behavior Modification Program, 1601 West Broad St., Columbus, Ohio 43223.

Description of a behavioral intervention project for autistic, mentally retarded, and emotionally disturbed children, ten years of age or younger, involving the training of parent-volunteer workers to carry out the therapeutic, re-educative process in the home. The goals, problems, implementation, evaluation, and parent-volunteer recruitment and training program are reviewed and discussed along with detailed case studies of children and parents involved in the project.

165. Youth Development Center, University of Hawaii. *Program in behavior modification: Programs and results.* The School of Social Work, Youth Development Center, 1395 Lower Campus Rd., University of Hawaii, Honolulu, Hawaii 96822, 1969. 135 pp. $2.00 paper.

Consists of nine papers by outstanding contributors that were presented at a conference sponsored by the University of Hawaii in 1969, concerned with applications of behavior modification in a variety of settings with particular focus on child, school, and family mental health. Included are discussions of the use of behavior modification in: multi-problem families; oppositional children and parental interactions; academic, social, and self-care problems of disadvantaged youth; management of classroom behaviors; and work with adolescent delinquents and neurotics. These presentations would be useful as reading material in staff development and other inservice training courses for mental health staff and personnel.

Applications in Special Settings for Children and Youth 4

---

166. Abrams, J. C. and Gordon, M. Teaching the delinquent child in a residential setting. *Journal of Reading,* 1969, *12,* 471-478. Available from Dr. Jules C. Abrams, Director, Institute for Learning, Hahnemann Medical College, Philadelphia, Pennsylvania 19102.

Report on the effect of varying conditions of reinforcement on increasing the quantity and level of reading among different groups of boys in the Youth Development Center, a residential center for delinquents in Philadelphia. The most successful group was the one that received reinforcement for the quality (90 percent comprehension) and quantity of extra reading. The authors discuss some of the problems and implications of their work.

167. Ashem, B. A. and Poser, E. G. *Behavior modification with children.* Pergamon Press, Inc., Maxwell House, Fairview Park, Elmsford, New York 10523, 1972. In press.

A major purpose of this volume is to provide a comprehensive source book for all personnel in mental health, education, and related fields who work with children in schools, families, hospitals, clinics, and the community in general. The book is divided into four major sections and consists of 41 articles and papers concerned with applications of behavior modification to: (1) relatively normal children who have particular problems such as speech and language handicaps, reading difficulties, anxiety, and other school adjustment problems, etc.; (2) emotionally disturbed children, e.g., phobias, anorexia nervosa, disruptive, destructive behaviors, social isolation, etc.; and (3) autistic, schizophrenic, retarded, and organic dysfunctional children. The fourth section of the book is concerned with training various agents of change for children—both professional and nonprofessional—including teachers, parents, adult volunteers, etc. This book will be a useful reference for professional workers in child mental health and related areas.

168. Bailey, J. S., Wolf, M. M., and Phillips, E. L. Home-based reinforcement and the modification of predelinquents' classroom behavior. *Journal of Applied Behavior Analysis*, 1970, *3*, 223-233. Available from Dr. Jon S. Bailey, Department of Psychology, Florida State University, Tallahassee, Florida 32306.

Report of a study to increase classroom performance of five boys, ages eleven to fifteen, who were residents of Achievement Place—a home-style, residential program for predelinquent boys in Lawrence, Kansas. All of these boys were low achievers, three had been labeled "school behavior problems" by their teachers, and two were described as "uncontrollable." The study was carried out in a special summer school math class; each boy had a "report card" that was marked daily by the teacher with either "yes" or "no," depending on whether he had studied the whole period and followed all the classroom rules. "Yeses" earned privileges in the home while a "no" resulted in a loss of all privileges in the home. The authors conclude that home-based reinforcement can be a very effective and practical classroom behavior modification technique. See Phillips, 181, for extensive material on the Achievement Place approach to delinquents.

169. Bensberg, G. J. (Ed.) *Teaching the mentally retarded: A handbook for ward personnel.* Southern Regional Education Board, 130 Sixth St. N. W., Atlanta, Georgia 30313, 1965. $1.75 paper.

Although this manual was written for personnel who work with mentally retarded children in residential settings, much of it would be useful to parents, teachers, and child care workers in general. It is divided into two sections: (1) developmental behavior patterns of normal and retarded children; general principles for teaching social, motor, and language skills; and the planning and evaluation of a cooperative training program; and (2) the use of operant reinforcement procedures and behavior shaping techniques in the development of a variety of self-care, self-help, and related skills. A film, *Teaching the Mentally Retarded—A Positive Approach*, was produced for use with this manual; see film section, 211.

170. Birnbrauer, J. S., Wolf, M. M., Kidder, J. D., and Tague, C. E. Classroom behavior of retarded pupils with token reinforcement. *Journal of Experimental Child Psychology*, 1965, *2*, 219-235. Available from Dr. Jay S. Birnbrauer, Department of Psychology, University of North Carolina, Chapel Hill, North Carolina 27514.

Report on a study of 17 mildly to moderately retarded children, ages eight to fourteen, enrolled in the Rainier School Programmed Learning Classroom for the retarded in Buckley, Washington. The token system consisted of check marks which the teachers recorded in individual booklets of each pupil. These check marks, which were earned for specified academic achievement and other desired behaviors, were exchangeable for back-up reinforcements that included a variety of tangible items (candies, toys, etc.) at the end of each school day. This token reinforcement system was studied in terms of the effects of discontinuing it for relatively long periods of time (21 to 35 days), followed by reinstatement of the system. Results indicate the effectiveness of operant behavior modification with such children in programmed classroom settings.

171. Browning, R. M. and Stover, D. O. *Behavior modification in child treatment.* Aldine, Atherton, Inc., 529 South Wabash Ave., Chicago, Illinois 60605, 1971. 422 pp. $11.95.

Based on the applied research behavior modification intensive residential treatment project of the Wisconsin Children's Treatment Center in Madison. The first half of the book is concerned with basic principles, methods and procedures, techniques of treatment, description of the treatment center, etc., while the second half is concerned with five case studies: four young psychotic children and one older child—all of whom had multiple and marked behavior problems including autism, speech, toilet, sleeping and eating difficulties, tantrums, noncompliance, aggressions, etc. Step-by-step applications of operant-behavior modification to these children are thoroughly described. A unique component of the project was the training of the parents in behavior modification and child management so that they could carry out and continue the therapeutic process in the homes and within the families of these severely disturbed children. Ethical considerations, the use of punishment, tokens, role playing, modeling and imitation, etc., in behavior modification are discussed.

172. Burchard, J. D. Community based behavior modification programs for the prevention of juvenile delinquency: Some strategies for intervention. Paper presented at a Workshop on Delinquency Treatment Models, University of North Carolina at Charlotte, Charlotte, North Carolina, 1972. Available from Dr. John D. Burchard, Department of Psychology, University of Vermont, Burlington, Vermont 05401.

Preliminary report on two behavior modification projects being carried out through a delinquency prevention agency in Burlington, Vermont. The first project involves three intervention programs: (1) a Big Brother model, (2) a behavior modification model, and (3) a control or "whatever develops" group. A total of 128 male and female adolescents, ages twelve to fifteen, and matched in terms of such variables as truancy, school suspension, stealing, property damage, police contacts, etc., are being studied to determine the relative effectiveness of these programs. The objective of the behavior modification program is to train teachers, parents, and other significant adults in the lives of these youths to use natural reinforcers and contingency management principles in reducing delinquent and increasing prosocial behaviors. The second project is concerned with a behavioral analysis training program designed to improve the relationships between police and youth particularly in spontaneous, stressful situations. Since both these projects are in progress, the author's discussion is based on planning, early implementation, and initial impressions. For other contributions of the author concerned with delinquents, see Burchard, J. and Tyler, V., Jr., The modification of delinquent behavior through operant conditioning. *Behaviour Research and Therapy*, 1965, *2*, 245-250; and Burchard, J. and Barrera, F., The analysis of time out and response cost in a programmed environment for delinquent retardates. *Journal of Applied Behavior Analysis*, 1972, in press.

173. Cohen, H. L. and Filipczak, J. *A new learning environment.* Jossey-Bass, Inc., 615 Montgomery St., San Francisco, California 94111, 1971. 192 pp. $8.75.

This book, with forewords by R. Buckminster Fuller and B. F. Skinner, describes and summarizes the results of a one-year experimental residential program involving 41 juvenile delinquents—approximately half black and half white—with a mean age of about 17 years. The purpose of the project, which was carried out at the National Training School for Boys in Washington, D.C. in 1966-1967, was to study the effectiveness of an operant behavioral modification environment in increasing the academic achievements and social skills of this group of so-called, "hardened" delinquent youth—all of whom had been long-term school failures. The project, known as CASE (Contingencies Applicable to Special Education), successfully demonstrated the powerful effects of a contingency reinforcement environment in bringing about marked positive changes in the behavior of these youth—as much as four grade levels, in positive attitudinal changes, and in IQ as much as 27 points. Although based on delinquents in a 24-hour institutional facility, this material has significant implications not only for correctional officials and programs, but for teachers and others who work with children and youth in educational settings. For a brief account of the CASE project, see Programming educational behavior for institutionalized adolescents. In H. C. Rickard (Ed.), *Behavioral intervention in human problems.* Pergamon Press, Inc., Maxwell House, Fairview Park, Elmsford, New York 10523, 1971. Pp. 179-200, $19.50. Also see film section, 213, for H. L. Cohen's *Contingencies Applicable to Special Education-CASE II.*

174. DeRisi, W. J. Performance contingent parole: A behavior modification system for juvenile offenders. Paper presented at the Annual Meeting of the American Psychological Association, Washington, D. C., 1971. Available from Dr. William J. DeRisi, Box 6000, Northern California Youth Center, Stockton, California 95206.

Report on a four-year behavior modification treatment and research program at one of the California Youth Authority's institutions for delinquent boys, ages fifteen to twenty-one, (Karl Holton School for Boys, Stockton, California). The major component of this program is a form of performance-contingent parole based on three main goal-directed behaviors: (1) appropriate institutional behaviors, (2) academic achievements, and (3) critical behavior deficiencies. Weekly written contingency contracts are used for each boy who is able to earn points referred to as Behavior Change Units (BCU) for specified behaviors and levels of performance in these three categories. Supervisors in the program evaluate all line staff members on the percentage of boys under contingency contract and on quality-of-contract requirements. The author summarizes the overall effectiveness and problems of the behavioral contingent parole approach with delinquents.

175. Giles, D. K., Tsosie, P., and Harris, V. W. Southwest Indian youth center. Program, Research and Evaluation Reports, 1971. Material available from Dr. David K. Giles, Executive Director, Southwest Indian Youth Center, Box 2266, Tucson, Arizona 85702.

These reports describe the overall program of a behavior modification treatment approach for delinquent Indian boys, ages thirteen to twenty-one. Most of these boys were from poverty-stricken reservation communities, broken homes, or alcoholic families; psychosocial problems in these boys consisted of drinking, truancy, academic failures, deficient work skills, sniffing paint, out-of-control behaviors in the home, school, and community. The program was established in 1970 at Mt. Lemmon near Tucson, Arizona, as a residential-institutional facility but has subsequently moved more to community-based residences or halfway houses in Tucson. Each residence has six to eight boys and one or two group-life supervisors; currently, there are 80 boys in the total program—about half in the institutional center and half in the community homes. Operant reinforcement systems are used to decrease disruptive behaviors and to increase appropriate behaviors and academic achievements. On the basis of the first year and a half of this demonstration project, the authors conclude that the behavior modification model offers an effective, economical, exportable alternative to traditional "correctional" institutional approaches to delinquent Indian youth.

176. Hamilton, J. Environmental control and retardate behavior. In H. C. Rickard (Ed.), *Behavioral intervention in human problems.* Pergamon Press, Inc., Maxwell House, Fairview Park, Elmsford, New York 10523, 1971. Pp. 383-409 $19.50.

Discussion of an experimental operant reinforcement program for some 300 moderately, severely, and profoundly retarded females, children, adolescents, and adults in five cottages at the Gracewood State School and Hospital, Gracewood, Georgia. The author describes the establishment of this program and the necessity of changing traditional management and treatment philosophies and practices concerning institutionalized retardates. Case examples; controlling specific problem behaviors; facilitating developmental skills, e.g., toilet training, feeding, and self-care with profoundly retarded females; the use of social reinforcement; sheltered workshops; and parental involvement are discussed within the behavior modification framework of this project.

177. Hobbs, N. Helping disturbed children: Psychological and ecological strategies. *American Psychologist*, 1966, *21*, 1105-1115. Available from Dr. Nicholas Hobbs, Provost, Vanderbilt University, Nashville, Tennessee 37203.

In this paper the author, who was responsible for the conceptualization, planning, and establishment of the original Re-Ed Model and residential schools in Tennessee and North Carolina for emotionally disturbed children, describes the development, philosophy, goals, and distinctive characteristics of the Re-Education approach. This involves a social-behavioral-ecological-relearning approach in contrast to the traditional clinical-intrapsychic-psychotherapeutic approach to disturbed, or so-called, "mentally ill" children. The Re-Ed Residential School Programs for Children, initiated by Hobbs in a demonstration grant from the National Institute of Mental Health in 1961, have been adopted by the Tennessee Department of Mental Health and represent a major component of that state's treatment services for children. See other papers in this section by Lewis, 178; Rousseau, 184; Weinberg, 188; and Weinstein, 189, for material on the Re-Ed Program.

178. Lewis, W. W. Project Re-Ed: The program and a preliminary evaluation. In H. C. Rickard (Ed.), *Behavioral intervention in human problems.* Pergamon Press, Inc., Maxwell House, Fairview Park, Elmsford, New York 10523, 1971. Pp. 79-100 $19.50.

Presents a brief history, overview, and evaluation of the Re-Ed Residential Programs for emotionally disturbed children in Tennessee and North Carolina. Describes the kinds of children and the process of how children are referred to the Re-Ed school, the day-to-day Re-Ed schedule of activities, the selection and training of staff, the functions of different staff members, etc. Presents evaluative data on the first 250 children who were involved in the Re-Ed Programs. The author concludes that this model provides an effective and relatively economical means of helping disturbed children on a short term residential basis. For additional material on the Re-Ed approach, see the following papers in this section: Hobbs, 177; Rousseau, 184; Weinberg, 188, and Weinstein, 189.

179. Lovaas, O. I., Koegel, R., Simmons, J' Q., and Stevens, J. Some generalization and follow-up measures on autistic children in behavior therapy. *Journal of Applied Behavior Analysis*, 1972, in press. Available from Dr. O. Ivar Lovaas, Department of Psychology, University of California at Los Angeles, Los Angeles, California 90024.

This material provides a summary of the pioneering work of Lovaas and his colleagues with 20 severely psychotic, autistic children at UCLA over the past five years. The basic approach involved operant reinforcement therapy and behavior modification procedures and focused on speech, social, and self-help skills. The five, measurable, behavioral categories whose presence or absence were used to describe these autistic children included: (1) self-stimulation-stereotyped repetitive behavior (rocking, spinning, gazing, etc.); (2) echolalic and other bizarre speech; (3) appropriate speech; (4) social nonverbal behavior; and (5) appropriate play. Most of these children had been intentionally selected because they had the poorest prognosis and had been previously diagnosed as retarded and brain damaged in addition to being psychotic and autistic. Follow-up data are presented for ten children obtained between one and four years after termination of the behavioral treatment program. The authors summarize the overall results and discuss the strengths and advantages along with the weaknesses, problems, and implications in carrying out their approach. Note: Several of the same children described in this material appear in the Lovaas films: *Reinforcement Therapy*, 228, and *Behavior Modification: Teaching Language to Psychotic Children*, 227. Other papers on behavior modification with autistic, psychotic, and retarded children may be obtained from Dr. Lovaas as indicated above.

180. Osborne, J. G. and Wageman, R. M. Some operant conditioning techniques and their use in schools for the deaf. *American Annals of the Deaf*, 1969, *114*, 741-753. Available from Dr. J. Grayson Osborne, Department of Psychology, Utah State University, Logan, Utah 84321.

Description of the utilization of behavioral analysis and modification in working with deaf children at state schools for the deaf in New Mexico and Colorado including token, point, and Premack reinforcement techniques for dormitory children. Operant reinforcement principles are outlined and explained as follows: (1) strengthening existing behaviors through positive and negative reinforcement and avoidance conditioning; (2) maintaining existing behaviors; (3) establishing new behaviors through shaping and priming; (4) weakening or eliminating behaviors through extinction, punishment, and conditioning incompatible behaviors. Relevant applications are made of these procedures to a variety of behaviors in deaf children.

181. Phillips, E. L. Achievement Place: Token reinforcement procedures in a home-style rehabilitation setting for 'predelinquent' boys.

Journal of Applied Behavior Analysis, 1968, *1*, 213-223. Available from Dr. Elery L. Phillips, Bureau of Child Research, University of Kansas, Lawrence, Kansas 66044.

Report of a successful project involving three boys, ages twelve, thirteen, and fourteen, declared dependent-neglected by the county court, who resided in a community-based, home-style, rehabilitation setting in which the author and his wife served as house-parents. These boys, from low income families, had a history of stealing, fighting, truancy, disruptive behaviors, school failure, etc. A point reinforcement system, involving 3x5 cards for each boy, was used in which points were earned for specified appropriate behaviors, e.g., personal cleanliness, doing household tasks, reading books, maintaining desirable grades in school work, etc. and lost for specified inappropriate behaviors, e.g., aggressive behaviors, lack of cleanliness, using poor grammar, stealing, lying. The earned points could be exchanged for various reinforcements in the form of naturally available activities, e.g., riding bicycle, watching TV, snacks, staying up past bedtime, etc. The author concludes that this kind of behavioral reinforcement, home-based approach offers a basis for an effective and economical rehabilitation program for predelinquents. For later developments and more extensive accounts, See Phillips, E. L., Phillips, E. A., Fixsen, D. L., and Wolf, M. M. Achievement Place: Modification of the behaviors of pre-delinquent boys within a token economy. *Journal of Applied Behavior Analysis*, 1971, *4*, 45-59; *Achievement Place: A brief description, 1971*, a 24-page monograph; and The Achievement Place Project: A community-based behavior modification, peer-oriented alternative to institutionalization for troubled youth. Paper presented at a Workshop on Delinquency Treatment Models, University of North Carolina at Charlotte, Charlotte, North Carolina, 1972. These and related materials are available from Dr. Elery L. Phillips at the address indicated above.

182. Rickard, H. C. (Ed.) *Behavioral intervention in human problems.* Pergamon Press, Inc., Maxwell House, Fairview Park, Elmsford, New York 10523, 1971. 422 pp. $19.50.

This volume, with some 24 contributors, covers a wide range of programs for both children and adults and is concerned with the use of behavioral procedures in intervention, treatment, and rehabilitation. Specific programs for children and youth include: (1) behavioral-community approach to school phobias and other disorders; (2) brief survey of behavioral applications for teachers in the classroom; (3) the re-education residential approach to disturbed children; (4) behavior modification in a therapeutic summer camp for disturbed children and youth; (5) experimental educational, behaviorally-oriented applications to the classroom; (6) programmed behavioral and educational approaches to institutionalized adolescent and young offenders; and (7) behavioral procedures with institutionalized mentally retarded. This book would be useful as a reference source containing a number of significant, innovative intervention programs in mental health, education, and related disciplines.

183. Rickard, H. C. and Dinoff, M. Behavior modification in a therapeutic summer camp. In H. C. Rickard (Ed.), *Behavioral intervention in human problems.* Pergamon Press, Inc., Maxwell House, Fairview Park, Elmsford, New York 10523, 1971. Pp. 101-127 $19.50.

As co-director of Camp Ponderosa, a therapeutic summer camp for emotionally disturbed children and youth, the authors describe and summarize the use of behavior modification principles and group-oriented, problem-solving procedures in their program over a period of six summers. The establishment, philosophy, development, staffing, major objectives, and evaluation of this program are discussed. Also, see Dinoff, M. Camp Ponderosa: A Therapeutic Summer Camp for the Emotionally Disturbed Child. Paper presented at a symposium on Therapeutic Camping for Emotionally Disturbed Children, South Carolina Department of Mental Health, Columbia, South Carolina, 1971. Available from Dr. Michael Dinoff, Director, Psychological Clinic, University of Alabama, Box 6142, University, Alabama 35486.

184. Rousseau, F. Behavioral programming in the re-education school. Tennessee Department of Mental Health, 1971, 14 pp. Available from Child and Youth Development Institute, 3420 Richards St., Nashville, Tennessee 37215.

Discussion of the ecological-behavioral philosophy and treatment approaches used in the Re-Education Schools and Programs developed in Tennessee. Major topics covered include behavioral assessment and programming involving a ten-step outline of procedures, setting behavioral goals, contingency contracting, Premack Principle, the use of the peer group, token economies, and time out. For other papers on the Re-Ed Program in this section see Hobbs, 177; Lewis, 178; Weinberg, 188; and Weinstein, 189.

185. Tharp, R. G. and Wetzel, R. J. *Behavior modification in the natural environment.* Academic Press, 111 Fifth Ave., New York, New York 10003, 1969. 250 pp. $10.00.

Concerned with the principles and applications of behavior modification with children in terms of home and school settings. Also, discusses the limitations of the "illness" model in mental health work. The basis of this book was a two-year behavior research project directed by the authors which involved 147 male and female youth between six and sixteen years of age, most of whom had been referred by the two local participating school districts because of multiple behavioral disturbances, including theft, runaways, destructiveness, classroom disruption, defiance, academic underachievement, predelinquent and delinquent acts, etc. The primary intervention with these subjects involved the use of behavior modification, particularly the technique of contingency management, which was almost completely carried out by "behavior analysts"—a group of eight nontraditional behavior modification technicians (a former Peace Corps volunteer, housewife, sociology majors, ex-stevedore, and carpenter) who were specifically trained by the authors. These technicians worked in the home and in the schools of the children and served as consultants to the actual mediators of change, i.e., parents and teachers. Procedures for setting up a behavior modification program, problems involved, and many case examples are included. This book would be particularly helpful to mental health professionals in consultative work and in-service training with teachers, counselors, public health nurses, case workers, and others concerned with children and youth.

186. Ulrich, R., Stachnik, T., and Mabry, J. (Eds.) *Control of human behavior, Vol. II: From cure to prevention.* Scott, Foresman & Co., Glenview, Illinois 60025, 1970. 378 pp. $5.50 paper, $7.50 hard.

A collection of 60 papers concerned with the utilization of behavior modification procedures in various settings including mental hospitals, outpatient clinics, schools, family settings, correctional facilities, etc. Of particular concern to those who work with children and youth are papers on Contingencies Applicable to Special Education (CASE I); Achievement Place for Predelinquent Boys; Operant Reinforcement Programs for Mentally Retarded, Brain-injured, Deaf, Self-injuring, Hyperactive, Out-of-control, Disruptive Children and Youth. This volume covers applications of behavior modification in all kinds of settings with both children and adults with a large variety of behavioral disturbances and deficits. Approximately half of the papers have direct relevance for child mental health and constitute a helpful resource for work with teachers, parents, personnel in residential programs, and other workers concerned with children and youth.

187. Wasik, B. H. and Steinke, P. L. Janus House: A community-based residential home for delinquent boys. Prepublication paper, 1972. Available from Dr. Barbara H. Wasik, School of Education, University of North Carolina, Chapel Hill, North Carolina 27514.

Description of a home-type, residential center for delinquent boys referred by the courts as an alternative to commitment to a state "correctional" institution because of a variety of deviant, antisocial, or disruptive behaviors. This center, established in 1971 and located in the Chapel Hill-Hillsborough area of North Carolina, is patterned after the Achievement Place Model in Kansas (see Phillips, 181). Full-time "teaching-parents"—a professionally trained, married couple—are responsible for eight to ten boys in this community-based and community-controlled program that utilizes operant reinforcement principles and procedures. These boys are able to maintain daily contact in the community including the school system. Increased intervention and preventive work with both parents and teachers is planned for this program during the coming year.

188. Weinberg, S. (Ed.) *The Children's Re-Education Center: An overview.* **Available from Tennessee Department of Mental Health, Division of Children and Youth Services, 3420 Richards St., Nashville, Tennessee 37215, 1971. 47 pp. mimeographed.**

This material describes the structure, organization, and program of the Tennessee Re-Education Centers for Emotionally Disturbed Children, ages six to thirteen. These Centers operate on a five-day-a-week residential basis and serve as schools rather than hospitals; the therapeutic approach is based on a social-learning-ecological-behavioral model rather than a clinical or psychiatric model. The staff includes principal, teacher-counselors, community liaison counselors, curriculum supervisors, educational aides.   Although back-up consultation is provided by mental health and medical consultants, the entire Re-education Program is carried out by educational personnel. The focus is on helping children develop social, academic, and other competencies and learn the kinds of behaviors that will enable them to cope with their environments. A similar Re-education Residential Program for Emotionally Disturbed Adolescents, known as Pine Breeze, has also been established in Tennessee that shares the same philosophy of treatment and follows the same kind of program as that for children. See other papers in this section on the Re-Ed Residential Model: Hobbs, 177; Lewis, 178; Rousseau, 184; and Weinstein, 189.

189. Weinstein, L. Project Re-Ed Schools for Emotionally Disturbed Children: Effectiveness as viewed by referring agencies, parents, and teachers. *Exceptional Children*, **1969, *35*, 703-711. Available from Dr. Laura Weinstein, Department of Psychology, Peabody College for Teachers, Nashville, Tennessee 37203. Also in N. J. Long, W. C. Morse, and R. G. Newman (Eds.),** *Conflict in the Classroom* **(2nd Ed.). Wadsworth Publishing Co., Belmont, California 94002, 1971. Pp. 553-561. $5.95 paper.**

Descriptive report on the first 250 children who were residents of the two original Project Re-Ed Schools—Cumberland House in Nashville, Tennessee, and Wright School in Durham, North Carolina—short-term residential programs for school-age, preadolescent, emotionally disturbed children. Focus on this paper is on the effectiveness of the

Re-Education approach in terms of the behavioral and academic changes and improvements in this initial group of children as reported by their parents, schools, and referring agencies. See other papers in this section by Hobbs, 177; Lewis, 178; Rousseau, 184; and Weinberg, 188, for material on the Re-Ed Residential Model for emotionally disturbed and related handicapped children.

Applications in Marriage and Family Counseling

5

190. Carter, R. D. and Thomas, E. J. Modification of problematic marital communication using corrective feedback and instruction. *Behavior Therapy*, 1972, in press. Available from Dr. Robert D. Carter, School of Social Work, University of Michigan, Ann Arbor, Michigan 48104.

Reports on the exploratory use of a Corrective Feedback and Instructions (CF-I) approach with nine couples having problems in marital communications. Involved in this approach is an electromechanical Signal System for the Assessment and Modification of Behavior, "SAM." The nine couples reported on in this paper completed a series of three one-and-one-half-hour tape-recorded sessions during which they engaged in conversation with each other that included such relevant topics as "Problems You Have in Your Marriage" and "Expectations of Each Other as Husband and Wife." Analysis was made of each couple's verbal interactions and feedback provided for further conversations, focus on specific problems in communication, and specific behavioral intervention procedures for improving the marital interaction. The authors discuss the usefulness of the communication-feedback-instructional model in terms of data presented on four of the couples who participated. See also Thomas, E. J., Carter, R. D., and Gambrill, E. D. Some possibilities of behavioral modification of marital problems using "SAM" (Signal System for the Assessment and Modification of Behavior). In R. D.Rubin, H. Fensterheim, A. A. Lazarus, and C. M. Franks (Eds.), *Advances in behavior therapy, 1969*. Academic Press, 111 Fifth Ave., New York N. Y., 10003, 1971. Pp. 273-287 $14.50.

191. Fielding, L. T. *The modification of human behavior*. Oakdale Medical Center, Suite 309, Minneapolis, Minnesota 55422, 1969. Forty programmed chapters $4.25 mimeographed.

This self-instructional, programmed text was designed to help individuals with no background or training in mental health learn how to apply behavior modification procedures in their own lives and relationships with others. There are eight sections, each with five chapters, that are separated by task-oriented worksheets allowing for a maximum of individual application. The major principles and techniques in behavior modification are covered in a step-by-step manner and illustrated with numerous examples many involving marriage, family, parent-child, and other everyday human relationships. This manual of applied behavior modification would be useful in training courses with couples, family members, etc., as well as in individual counseling work.

192. Gambrill, E. D., Carter, R. D., and Thomas, E. J. Behavioral intervention in families: Notes and bibliography. *Social Work Education Reporter*, 1971, *19*, 46-49. Available from Dr. Eileen D. Gambrill, School of Social Welfare, University of California, Berkeley, California 94720.

Brief survey of some of the references in the literature concerned with the use of behavior modification procedures in disturbed parent-child, family, and marital interactions. The author concludes that such procedures may contribute significantly to the available interpersonal methods of family intervention in social work and merit the serious attention of social work educators and practitioners.

193. Goldiamond, I. Self-control procedures in personal behavior problems. *Psychological Reports*, 1965, *17*, 851-868. Available from Dr. Israel Goldiamond, Department of Psychiatry, University of Chicago, Chicago, Illinois 60637.

A discussion of operant reinforcement procedures in which a person learns to specify the particular behavior in himself to be changed and then to set up the conditions which facilitate the desired modification of that behavior. Applications are discussed both in terms of individual problem behaviors and two marriage counseling cases. See also the author's Justified and unjustified alarm over behavioral control in O. Milton and R. G. Wahler (Eds.), *Behavior disorders: Perspectives and trends* (2nd Ed.). J. B. Lippincott, East Washington Sq., Philadelphia, Pennsylvania 19105, 1969. Pp. 220-245 $5.25 paper.

194. Goldstein, M. K. and Francis, B. Behavior modification of husbands by wives. Paper presented at the Annual Meeting of the National Council on Family Relations, Washington, D. C., 1969. Available from Dr. Mark K. Goldstein, Department of Clinical Psychology, University of Florida, Gainesville, Florida 32601.

Report of a pilot study of a group of five wives of graduate students who participated in a project concerned with the applicability of behavior modification to changes in interspousal behaviors. These wives met as a group once a week with a mental health consultant over a period of several weeks. Each wife selected a specific, current, recurring behavior of her husband that she had previously attempted to change but without success, e.g., drinking too much beer, leaving clothes on floor, lack of affectionate communication, etc. Applications of behavior analysis and operant reinforcement principles were discussed by the consultant and carried out by these wives. The authors discuss the positive results of this study in terms of the use of behavioral procedures by couples in improving their own marital relationship, as well as the use of such procedures by one spouse when the other spouse is not involved in marriage counseling.

195. Knox, D. *Marriage happiness: A behavioral approach to counseling.* Research Press, Box 3177 Country Fair Station, Champaign, Illinois 61820, 1971. 171 pp. $4.00 paper.

This book was written primarily for mental health professionals, marriage counselors, and others who work with cases in which a major source of difficulty is in the marital relationship. The frame of reference is broadly behavioral and includes a number of techniques and procedures used in behavior modification: operant reinforcement, systematic desensitization, assertive training, modeling, aversive conditioning, extinction, Premacking, behavioral contracts, etc. The book is divided into three parts: (1) behavioral procedures; (2) applications to common problems in marriage (sex, communication, in-laws, alcohol, children, money, etc.); and (3) actual marriage counseling cases in which behavioral procedures were used. Appendices include a marriage inventory, instructions for learning how to relax, and the use of an electric vibrator to facilitate orgasmic responses.

196. Liberman, R. Behavioral approaches to family and couple therapy. *American Journal of Orthopsychiatry*, 1970, *40*, 106-118. Available from Dr. Robert Liberman, Research Unit, Camarillo State Hospital, Box A, Camarillo, California 93010.

Discusses the successful application of behavior modification in marriage and family therapy. Four cases are described in which behavioral analysis is effectively and successfully utilized by means of an educational rather than clinical approach: (1) the problems are specified in observable terms, (2) the goals for marital or familial improvement are established, and (3) contingencies of reinforcement are arranged to produce the desired changes in interpersonal relations in the marital or family unit. Demonstration of the use of behavioral analysis and modification in marriage counseling.

197. Miller, L. M., Erickson, M., James, R. E., Jr., Knox, D., Lawrence, S., and Schroader, C. *Family behavior seminar: A course in behavioral*

science to improve family discipline, motivation, and academic and professional achievement, 1972. Information about this course, cost, etc., available from Human Behavior Institute, Box 25025, Raleigh, North Carolina 27611.

This is an 18-lesson cassette tape seminar or course in behavior modification principles and procedures with focus on individual, parent-child, marital, and family applications. Examples of specific lesson topics include: (1) Tools of Behavior Change, (2) Planning Behavior Change, (3) The Preschool Years, (4) Childhood Problems, (5) The Teenager and His Family, (6) Parent Support of Learning, (7) Behavior and Marriage Success, etc. This material has been designed for use by individual families as well as mental health and related professional workers.

198. Miller, W. H. Direct family intervention: Cases and issues. Prepublication monograph, 1972. Information available from Dr. William H. Miller, Center for the Health Sciences and Neuropsychiatric Institute, University of California at Los Angeles, Los Angeles, California 90024.

The author's Direct Family Intervention Approach, which is based on behavior modification principles and procedures, is outlined and described in detail in this material. Included are: (1) glossary of terms and concepts relevant to behavioral intervention techniques; (2) nine programs that presently constitute the family intervention process: (a) reading material on behavior modification (*Living with Children* by Patterson and Gullion or *Families* by Patterson), (b) understanding operant reinforcement, (c) home contingencies, (d) time-out procedures, (e) re-engineering or trying new home contingencies, (f) didactic-supportive sessions for family members, (g) desensitization-relaxation procedures, (h) assertive training, and (i) use of modeling by the therapist; (3) flo-chart showing the entire Direct Family Intervention Program and how it is carried out; (4) case examples of six families with whom the intervention process was conducted; and (5) appendices including various materials, checklists, data sheets, etc., utilized in the program. Videotape feedback is used as an aid in the training of parents in operant techniques. Preliminary results indicate that this systematic, behavioral approach to family counseling holds considerable promise and merits further consideration and evaluation.

199. Patterson, G. R. *Families: Applications of social learning to family life.* Research Press, Box 3177 Country Fair Station, Champaign, Illinois 61820, 1971. 143 pp. $3.00 paper

A practical guide to the understanding and use of various behavioral procedures in parent-child, husband-wife, and other family relationships including adolescents and the parents themselves. This book, which is based on the author's extensive clinical work and applied research with both normal and problem families, is semi-programmed in format, written in very clear, understandable language, and replete with examples from everyday life and family living. The emphasis is on practical applications in family relations and on parents as "behavior managers." Would be a valuable resource and aid for mental health and related personnel to use in parent-child, family, and marital counseling.

200. Patterson, G. R. and Hops, H. Coercion, a game for two: Intervention techniques for marital conflict. In R. E. Ulrich and P. Mountjoy (Eds.), *The experimental analysis of social behavior*. Appleton-Century-Crofts, 440 Park Ave., South, New York, New York 10016, 1972. In press.

Discussion of marital disturbances and conflicts in terms of coercive interchanges in which the spouses provide aversive stimuli and consequences that control the behavior of each other; these coercive interactions are maintained by the reinforcement that results from termination of the aversively stimulating conditions, i.e., the reinforcement resulting from the termination of aversive marital exchanges strengthens the coercive behavior of both parties. Conflict involves an interchange in which one spouse does not comply with the demands for immediate changes in behavior made by the other. The authors report on their behavior modification intervention approach with a couple whose marital relationship had deteriorated over a three-year period. This consisted of training the couple in pinpointing behaviors to be changed, deciding on consequences for failure to comply, and setting up behavioral contracts for decelerating displeasing and accelerating pleasing behaviors in each other. Videotaped interactions including modeled interchanges were used in the marriage counseling invervention. Results suggest the feasibility of such a behavioral-reinforcement counseling-training approach to marital conflict and unhappiness. See also Hops, H., Wills, T., Weiss, R., and Patterson, G. R., Marital interaction coding system, unpublished manuscript, 1971. Available from Department of Psychology, University of Oregon, Eugene, Oregon 97403.

201. Rappaport, A. F. and Harrell, J. A behavioral-exchange model for marital counseling, unpublished manuscript, 1971. 61 pp. mimeographed. Available from Dr. Alan F. Rappaport, Family Consultation Center, College of Human Development, The Pennsylvania State University, University Park, Pennsylvania 16802.

The authors describe their Behavioral-Exchange-Educational Model in counseling couples with marital conflicts and disturbed relations. This model is based on operant behavior modification counseling procedures in which a married couple are first helped to establish a hierarchy of pinpointed, undesirable behaviors in each other together with the reinforcements that have maintained such unwanted behaviors in the past. Deceleration begins with the least disturbing, undesirable behaviors and proceeds progressively to the more serious and disruptive behaviors. In addition, each spouse prepared a hierarchy of positive or desirable behaviors manifested by the other. Behavioral-exchange contracts are drawn up by the couple to reciprocally eliminate or reduce targeted, undesirable behaviors and replace them with desirable ones. The case of a married couple is presented to illustrate how this approach in marriage counseling is carried out. The authors conclude with a discussion of the advantages along with precautions in the implementation of their model.

202. Rose, S. D. A behavioral approach to the group treatment of parents. *Social Work*, 1969, *14*, 21-29. Available from Dr. Sheldon D. Rose, School of Social Work, University of Michigan, Ann Arbor, Michigan 48104.

Report on behavioral counseling by second year graduate students in social work at the University of Michigan with small groups of parents (three to eight members) on a once-a-week basis for a period that ranged from five to sixteen weeks. Most of these parents were in the lower socioeconomic class and were seen in public agencies. The focus of the behavioral, small-group counseling was on helping parents cope with the behavioral problems of their children; major techniques utilized included programmed instruction, counselor modeling, behavioral rehearsal, and behavioral assignments. Results of this demonstration project were favorable and suggested further consideration of this approach in parent and family counseling.

203. Stuart, R. B. Behavioral contracting within the families of delinquents. *Journal of Behavior Therapy and Experimental Psychiatry*, 1971, *2*, 1-11. Available from Dr. Richard B. Stuart, School of Social Work, University of Michigan, Ann Arbor, Michigan 48104.

A thorough discussion of the utilization of behavioral contracts to improve relationships between delinquents and their families and schools. The author defines a behavioral contract in terms of specify ing the exchange of positive reinforcements among two or more persons and as involving four assumptions: (1) exchanged positive reinforcements are a privilege rather than a right; (2) effective agreements are based on reciprocity; (3) the value and usefulness of exchanges are a function of the range, rate, and magnitude of the positive reinforcements involved; and (4) contract rules create freedom in interpersonal exchanges. The case of a sixteen-year-old delinquent girl and her parents is described to illustrate the effective use of a behavioral contract. Various considerations, advantages, and problems in the use of contracts are discussed.

204. Stuart, R. B. Operant-interpersonal treatment for marital discord. *Journal of Consulting and Clinical Psychology*, 1969, *33*, 675-682. Available from Dr. Richard B. Stuart, School of Social Work, University of Michigan, Ann Arbor, Michigan 48104.

Discusses the successful application of behavior modification procedures in marriage counseling with four couples who were considering divorce. Each couple was seen for seven sessions over a ten-week period. Procedures included: (1) marital discord explained as problems in interpersonal behavior rather than intrapsychic illness, (2) behaviors to be accelerated in each spouse specified and frequency recorded, and (3) each spouse provided regular reinforcements of desired behaviors in the other. This paper demonstrates the applicability of behavior modification in marriage counseling.

205. Tharp, R. G. and Otis, G. D. Toward a theory for therapeutic intervention in families. *Journal of Consulting Psychology*, 1966, *30*, 426-434. Available from Dr. Roland G. Tharp, Department of Psychology, University of Hawaii, Honolulu, Hawaii 96822.

Psychosocial analysis of marriage and family problems and conflicts in terms of discrepancies between expectations of certain role behaviors and the actual enactment of these behaviors. Therapeutic intervention is based on the counselor's helping a couple, or family members, establish a quid pro quo system of "I'll change this if you change that." The modification of role behaviors through negotiation, sanctions, agreed upon efforts, etc., is accomplished by the family members carrying out these strategies in their daily lives. The authors discuss three cases involving marital discord and family conflict in terms of their role behavior modification approach.

206. Thomas, E. J. and Carter, R. D. Instigative modification with a multi-problem family. *Social Casework*, 1971, *52*, 444-454. Available from Dr. Edwin J. Thomas, School of Social Work, University of Michigan, Ann Arbor, Michigan 48104.

Report on the use and evaluation of behavior modification procedures in social welfare work with specific focus on "multi-problem families" that are referrals to and from a variety of community, welfare, and other agencies including schools, mental hospitals, mental health and child guidance centers, correctional programs, etc. Applications, problems, and implications of the behavioral model are discussed with reference to a specific multi-problem family from whom data analysis was completed.

207. Turner, A. J. Behavior modification as applied to marriage. Paper presented at the First Annual Meeting of the Rocky Mountain Behavior

Modification Conference, Denver, Colorado, 1972. Available from Dr. A. Jack Turner, Huntsville-Madison County Mental Health Center, 218 Randolph Avenue, Huntsville, Alabama 35801.

The author describes his Marriage Management Program developed in 1971-1972 and currently being carried out and evaluated at the Huntsville-Madison County Mental Health Center. The program involves groups of married couples and consists of six two-hour sessions of counseling as follows: (1) orientation to and applications of behavior modification procedures; (2) practice in pinpointing and recording actual behaviors; (3) use of behavioral contracts, token reinforcement systems, etc.; and (4, 5, and 6) review of day-to-day applications of behavioral procedures, successful cases, problems, discussion of making marriage more successful in terms of applications of behavioral principles. Each couple pays $60.00 for the course and enters into a contract whereby they can earn $30.00 back by attending each session, carrying out assigned tasks, etc. Materials used include: the marriage inventory, precounseling inventory, study questions for each session, examples of behavior contracts in marriage, and behavior record and charting forms. Within this Marriage Management Program, the author is exploring the relative advantages of group marriage counseling with both partners, focusing only on positive behaviors in each partner, and the use of a husband-wife therapist team versus only a single therapist in carrying out the program. Preliminary results are quite encouraging as to the effectiveness of this behavioral approach to marriage counseling.

208. Weathers, L., Liberman, R., and Allen, P. A natural environment approach to contingency contracting with soft drug abusing adolescents and their families. Unpublished manuscript, 1972. Information available from Dr. Lawrence Weathers, Research Assistant, Camarillo State Hospital, Camarillo, California 93010.

Concerned with the behavioral treatment of adolescent drug abuse, school problems, delinquency, and family problems in the natural setting of the home. The family receives a four-part intervention package: (1) a simulation game is used to develop a contingency contract between the adolescent and his family; (2) a portable, four channel bug-in-the-ear unit is used to teach family communication skills; (3) a card exchange cueing system is initiated to teach family members to recognize and reinforce prosocial behaviors in other family members; and (4) video tape feedback is used to shape family interaction skills. Data is collected through home observations, telephone contacts, school records, probation records, family behavioral checklists, etc.

209. Weiss, R. L. and Patterson, G. R. Innovations in marital therapy. Paper presented at the Annual Meeting of the Western Psychological

Association, San Francisco, California, 1971. Available from Dr. Robert L. Weiss, Psychology Clinic, University of Oregon, Eugene, Oregon 97403.

A presentation of a behavior modification approach to marital conflict, stressing assessment of exchanged pleases and displeases between spouses. The results of behavioral coding of negotiation samples are presented indicating that, compared with baseline, couples significantly decreased their aversive behaviors directed toward the spouse and increased problem solving, positive behaviors. The coding system proved to be a useful procedure in counseling couples with marital conflicts.

Films 6

210. Baldwin, V. L. and Fredericks, H. D. *Help for Mark*. 17 minutes, 16 mm, Color, Sound, 1970. Rental $18.00. Available from Appleton-Century-Crofts Film Library, 267 West 25th St., New York, New York 10001.
Introductory training film in behavior modification for parents and teachers of retarded children. Although principles of behavior mdofication are explained and demonstrated to the mother of a moderately retarded child, this film would also be useful for parents and teachers of children with other handicapped conditions. Uses and advantages of behavioral training procedures are discussed.

211. Bensberg, G. J. and Colwell, C. N. *Teaching the mentally retarded—A positive approach*. 22 minutes, 16 mm, Black and White, Sound, 1967. No rental fee. Available from National Medical Audio Visual Center Annex, Station K, Atlanta, Georgia 30324.
Produced as a training aid for personnel who work with institutionalized, mentally retarded children, this film demonstrates how behavior modification procedures can be used to increase desirable, more adaptive behaviors and decrease undesirable, less mature behaviors in severely retarded children over a four-month training period. This film would also be useful for work with parents and teachers of children with various behavioral problems or deficits. Produced for use with the manual, *Teaching the mentally retarded: A handbook for ward personnel*, edited by G. J. Bensberg (see 169).

212. Bushell, D. *Behavioral analysis classroom*. 20 minutes, 16 mm, Color, Sound, 1970. Rental $2.50. Available from the University of Kansas, Bureau of Visual Instruction, 6 Bailey Hall, Lawrence, Kansas 66044.
Shows the use of behavior modification and token reinforcement procedures in several Follow-Through classrooms in public elementary

schools. Basic principles and step-by-step applications are covered, along with answers to a number of questions often asked by teachers unfamiliar with the behavioral model. Also shows the important role teacher aides and parent volunteers can have in helping the teacher carry out the program and in training other aides and volunteers; demonstrates the effectiveness of behavioral techniques in accelerating academic achievement of children, in many instances one to two grade levels above their age. Would be useful in training work with all parents, elementary school teachers, and others concerned with the development and education of children.

213. Cohen, H. L. *Contingencies applicable to special education—Case II.* 20 minutes, 16 mm, Black and White, Sound, 1966. Rental $15.00. Available from Institute for Behavioral Research, Inc., 2429 Linden La., Silver Spring, Maryland 20910.

Shows several major aspects of the Case II residential behavior modification project concerned with 41 delinquents at the National Training School for Boys, Washington, D. C., 1966-67. Describes the use and effectiveness of operant reinforcement procedures in increasing academic achievement and prosocial behavior in delinquent youth. See H. L. Cohen and J. Filipczak's book, *A new learning environment*, San Francisco, Cal.: Jossey-Bass, 1971, for description and results of the Case II Project, (see 173).

214. Cohen, H. L. and Filipczak, J. *PREP: Preparation through responsive educational programs.* 12 minutes, 16 mm., Color, Sound, 1972. Rental $25.00. Available from Institute for Behavioral Research, Inc., 2429 Linden La., Silver Spring, Maryland 20910.

Provides a general overview of a highly individualized junior high school program designed for adolescents with social and academic problems. The four general components of the program are classroom-based interpersonal skills training, self-instructional academic training in English and mathematics, behavioral and academic follow-up of student activities in regular school classes, and a training program for parents of the students. A handbook that provides a detailed description of the PREP project has been prepared for use with this film; 20 copies are supplied with each rental.

215. Cohen, S. I. and Brown, W. L. *The ABC's of behavioral education: The use of behavior modification principles in education.* 18 minutes, 16 mm, Color, Sound, 1970. Rental $15.00. Available from Hallmark Films, Inc., 1511 E. North Ave., Baltimore, Maryland 21213.

Describes the behavior modification program at the Anne Arundel County Learning Center, Maryland. Emphasizes the relationships between A (antecedents), B (behavior), and C (consequences), and how the antecedents and consequences in the school environment can be programmed to increase prosocial and academic behaviors of students. The students at this center, ages twelve to seventeen, had been previously rejected or ejected from other schools throughout the county and had both social and academic deficits, histories of failure, punishment, frustrations, etc., in traditional school settings. The Arundel Learning Center's behavioral program was designed to provide a number of alternatives to students including a variety of appropriate curriculum materials, choice of reinforcers, freedom to remain outside of the work buildings, leave their study and work areas at any time, etc. This film demonstrates the effective use of operant reinforcement procedures within a special education and school setting.

216. CRM Productions. *Learning.* 26 minutes, 16 mm, Color, Sound, 1971. Rental $50.00. Available from CRM Films, 9263 Third St., Beverly Hills, California 90210.

This film covers several aspects of learning, imprinting, sign-stimuli, Pavlovian conditioning, and achievement motivation. The coverage of operant reinforcement and aversive conditioning includes interviews with Skinner, Azrin, and Malott. This film illustrates shaping the behavior of both rats and humans; instigating aggression in rats; teaching language to a mentally retarded child; and the conditioning, generalization, and later extinction of fear in a young child. Designed primarily for college and adult education courses in psychology.

217. Davison, G. C. and Krasner, L. *Behavior therapy with an autistic child.* 42 minutes, 16 mm, Black and White, Sound, 1964. No rental fee. Available from National Medical Audio-Visual Center Annex, Station K, Atlanta, Georgia 30324.

Demonstration of use of operant reinforcement procedures in increasing verbalizations and prosocial behaviors in an autistic, mentally retarded boy. Probably more useful for professional groups in mental health than with parents and teachers, especially those with little or no background in operant conditioning and principles of behavior modification.

218. Garmize, K. S., Garmize, L. M., and May, J. R. *Genesis.* 25 minutes, 16 mm, Color, Sound, 1971. Rental $20.00. Available from Hallmark Films, Inc., 1511 E. North Ave., Baltimore, Maryland 21213.

This is the first in a planned series of training films on the use of behavior modification procedures by those concerned with the care, teaching, and training of the mentally retarded. Self-instructional guide sheets are used with the film; these sheets contain questions that are sequentially programmed to the film and answered both visually and in the narration, thus facilitating the application on a step-by-step basis of the behavioral procedures presented in the film.

219. Graubert, P. *Dare to do.* 20 minutes, 16 mm, Black and White, Sound, 1971. Rental $50.00. Available from Synchro Films, Inc., 43 Bay Drive West, Huntington, New York 11743.

Shows the use of behavior modification procedures in a third grade class in a ghetto public school of New York City. Demonstrates the usefulness of operant reinforcement in changing the behaviors of students from a rejection of school to increased interest and achievement in the classroom.

220. Hall, R. V., Risley, T., and Wolf, M. *Spearhead at Juniper Gardens.* 38 minutes, 16 mm, Black and White, Sound, 1968. Rental $2.50. Available from University of Kansas, Bureau of Visual Instruction, 6 Bailey Hall, Lawrence, Kansas 66044.

Shows the Juniper Gardens Children's Program which is an applied research project concerned with providing a variety of services for children who live in a deprived area of northeast Kansas City, Kansas. One of the major services consists of two preschool classes and a remedial education class within the community, along with the training of public school teachers and parent-teaching assistants in the use of operant reinforcement procedures to decrease disruptive behaviors and increase language, academic, and prosocial behaviors in the children in the area. Would be useful in training courses both for parent and teacher groups.

221. Hall, R. V., Risley, T., and Wolf, M. *Teaching with tokens.* 8 minutes, 16 mm, Color, Sound, 1970. Rental $2.50. Available from University of Kansas, Bureau of Visual Instruction, 6 Bailey Hall, Lawrence, Kansas 66044.

Made at the Juniper Gardens Project Parent Cooperative Preschool, Kansas City, Kansas, this film presents a simple demonstration and review of rules in the use of tokens and social reinforcements in helping a child to learn to recognize objects, follow directions, attend to tasks, etc. Would be helpful as a training film for preschool and Head Start teachers and others concerned with the education of young children.

222. Herrnstein, R. J. and Morse, W. H. *Controlling behavior through reinforcement.* 16 minutes, 16 mm, Black and White, Sound, 1956. Rental $10.00. Available from McGraw-Hill Book Co., Film Department, 330 W. 42nd St., New York, New York 10036. Also available from Psychological Cinema Register, Audio-Visual Services, Pennsylvania State University, University Park, Pennsylvania 16802, rental $4.00; and from Extension Media Center, University of California, Berkeley, California 94720, rental $9.00.

Shows effect of varying reinforcement schedules on behavior of pigeons and compares results with similar demonstrations with children in an elementary school classroom. Designed for courses in learning, child and educational psychology, education, etc.

223. Herrnstein, R. J. and Morse, W. H. *Reinforcement in learning and extinction.* 8 minutes, 16 mm, Black and White, Sound, 1956. Rental $10.00. Available from McGraw-Hill Book Co., Film Department, 330 W. 42nd St., New York, New York 10036. Also available from Psychological Cinema Register, Audio-Visual Services, Pennsylvania State University, University Park, Pennsylvania 16802, rental $2.80; and from Extension Media Center, University of California, Berkeley, California 94720, rental $7.00.

Shows how the use of reinforcement establishes particular behaviors and nonreinforcement extinguishes behavior patterns. Laboratory demonstrations with pigeons are used and parallels are made to the behavior of children. Designed for courses in learning, child and educational psychology, education, etc.

224. Lent, J. and LeBlanc, J. *Operation behavior modification.* 37 minutes, 16 mm, Black and White, Sound, 1967. Rental $2.50. Available from the University of Kansas, Bureau of Visual Instruction, 6 Bailey Hall, Lawrence, Kansas 66044.

Demonstrates the use and effectiveness of an operant reinforcement program in training mentally retarded girls, ages eight to twenty-one, at the State Hospital and Training Center, Parsons, Kansas, for eventual functioning in a community environment. The establishment and implementation of a token reinforcement system to increase various adaptive resources including prosocial, self-care, occupational, homemaking, academic, and other behaviors. Although concerned only with mentally retarded children, this film would be useful for training work with parents, teachers, and other child care groups.

225. Lindsley, O. R. *Pinpoint, record and consequate.* 14 minutes, 16 mm, Color, Sound, 1967. Rental $25.00. Available from Behavior Research Company, P. O. Box 3351, Kansas City, Kansas 66103.

The use of behavior modification principles by parents in the home. The three steps: Pinpoint, Record, and Consequate are explained and illustrated by showing how parents used such contingencies as television programs to accelerate the learning of new words and to eliminate bed wetting. A practical demonstration of applications of behavioral analysis with children.

226. Lindsley, O. R. *Sunday box.* 14 minutes, 16 mm, Color, Sound, 1967. Rental $25.00. Available from Behavior Research Company, P. O. Box 3351, Kansas City, Kansas 66103.

A simple procedure of arranging natural consequences to eliminate littering in a home or office is demonstrated. A housewife and mother describes how she was able to use this approach in the elimination of littering in her family.

227. Lovaas, O. I. *Behavior modification: Teaching language to psychotic children.* 42 minutes, 16 mm, Color, Sound, 1969. Rental $30.00. Available from Appleton-Century-Crofts Film Library, 267 West 25th Street, N. W., New York, New York 10001. Also available from Bureau of Audiovisual Education, The University of North Carolina, 111 Abernathy Hall, Chapel Hill, North Carolina 27514, rental $13.00.

Demonstrates the use and effectiveness of operant behavior modification procedures in the development of speech and social behaviors with several severely autistic and psychotic children at the University of California in Los Angeles. This film is a revised and expanded version of the first part of the earlier film, *Reinforcement Therapy,* 228, produced in 1966 by Smith, Kline and French Laboratories. Would be useful in teaching behavioral procedures for use with various kinds of emotionally disturbed and other handicapped children.

228. Lovaas, O. I., Birnbrauer, J., and Schaefer, H. H. *Reinforcement therapy.* 45 minutes, 16 mm, Black and White, Sound, 1966. Rental $3.00 (2 days); $6.00 (1 week). Produced by Smith, Kline and French Laboratories and available from American Medical Association Film Library, 535 North Dearborn St., Chicago, Illinois 60610.

Demonstrates the use and effectiveness of operant behavior modification procedures in the development of speech and social behaviors in four severely autistic and psychotic children at the University of California at Los Angeles and academic and social skills in retarded children at the Rainier State School in Buckley, Washington. The third part deals with adult psychotics at Patton State Hospital, California. The first two-thirds of this film would be useful in teaching behavioral procedures for use with autistic, retarded, and other handicapped children.

229. Mager, R. F. *Who Did What To Whom?* 16½ minutes, Color, Sound, 1972. Information and brochure concerning this film available from Research Press Company, Box 3177 Country Fair Station, Champaign, Illinois 61820.

Designed as a training aid in work with parents, teachers, aides, and others to help them recognize basic behavioral principles in action and to provide practice in handling such situations successfully. Social learning principles included are positive and negative reinforcements, punishment, and extinction. Forty everyday scenes are depicted, e.g., home, school, and work settings. Should be used in conjunction with the *Leader's Guide* (included with the film) for a group training session approximately two hours in length. *Leader's Guide* by R. F. Mager includes complete film script, suggested questions for discussion, typical responses, scene summaries, and a list of necessary equipment for a group viewing session.

230. McBeath, M. and Seremeta, J. *PATCH—positive approach to changing humans: A training film for teachers.* 19 minutes, 16 mm, Color, Sound, 1970. Rental $25.00. Available from Shoreline Public Schools, Educational Service Center, N.E. 158th and 20th N.E., Seattle, Washington 98155. Also a manual to accompany this film, *A guide to PATCH for inservice leaders,* 1970, 36 pp. Available from Dr. Marcia McBeath at the same address.

This film was produced specifically for inservice teacher training in the use of behavior modification procedures to decrease disruptive and increase academic achievement behaviors in pupils. Contrasts are shown between unproductive and productive classroom situations based on the negative and positive effect of the behavior of teachers in relation to pupils. The focus throughout is on how teachers can apply operant reinforcement principles to enhance effective teaching and accelerate learning in the classroom. The accompanying film manual is based on five two-hour inservice teacher training sessions.

231. Meyerson, L. *Rewards and reinforcements in learning.* 26 minutes, 16 mm, Black and White, Sound, 1969. Rental $12.00. Available from Central Arizona Film Cooperative, Arizona State University, Tempe, Arizona 85281; and from Behavior Modification Productions, Box 3207, Scottsdale, Arizona 85257, rental $15.00 (3 days) plus $1.00 shipping charge and $1.00 for the study guide to accompany use of film. Also available from Extension Media Center, University of California, Berkeley, California 94720, rental $12.00.

Demonstrates the application and effectiveness of operant behavior modification procedures in helping a severely retarded child learn to walk and in helping nonmotivated elementary school pupils from poverty neighborhoods increase both their interest and achievement in academic subjects. Shows how to implement a token reinforcement system and use contingency management in classroom settings; covers normal as well as exceptional children of preschool and school age with particular focus on applications with disadvantaged children. The 44-page study guide is a valuable resource and would enhance the training effectiveness of this excellent film.

232. Nixon, S. *Behavior modification in the classroom.* 24 minutes, 16 mm, Black and White or Color, Sound, 1967. Rental $11.00 Black and

White, $16.00 Color. Available from Extension Media Center, University of California, Berkeley, California 94720. Also available from Santa Clara Unified School District, Santa Clara, California 95050, rental, $10.00 Black and White.

Based on earlier work of Patterson and others, this film demonstrates effective use of operant reinforcement, modeling, and behavioral role-playing procedures for teachers in three classroom situations: early, intermediate, and upper primary school levels. Shows pupil behaviors before and after intervention via behavior modification procedures. Primarily a teacher training film, although would be useful with all groups concerned with child and school mental health.

233. Palumbo, A. and Handyside, D. *Reward procedures for behavior management.* 25 minutes, 16 mm, Black and White, Sound, 1971. Rental $18.00. Available from Infomatics, Department A, 8531 Schaefer Highway, Detroit, Michigan 48228.

This film, which correlates with Kurtz and Palumbo's *The ABC's of Child Management, Workbook 1*, is one of a series of four instructional units concerned with teaching parents, teachers, child care workers, etc., how to carry out behavior modification procedures in home, school, and other settings. The focus of this particular film is on the nature, kinds, and applications of reinforcements that parents can use with elementary and high school age children, e.g., monetary, material, praise, point-check systems, use of privileges, behavioral contracts, etc. The other related films in the series include: *Reward Procedures for Classroom Management; Time Out: A Way to Help Children Behave*; and *Teaching Children New Behavior*. These films correlate with other workbooks by Kurtz and Palumbo (see 148). Each film is about 25 minutes, rents for $18.00, and is available from Infomatics as indicated above.

234. Reese, E. P. *Born to succeed.* Two reels: Reel 1, *The concept of number*, 32 minutes, 16 mm, Color, Sound. Reel 2, *Arithmetic*, 30 minutes, 16 mm, Color, Sound, 1971. Rental $55.00 both reels, or $30.00 one reel. Available from Appleton-Century-Crofts Film Library, 267 West 25th St., New York, New York 10001.

Shows the step-by-step application of operant reinforcement principles and procedures in teaching retarded children. Although concerned with helping the retarded child learn to conceptualize numbers and solve arithmetic problems, these films would be useful as training aids for parent and teacher training programs in general.

235. Reese, E. P. *Behavior theory in practice.* Four reels, 20 minutes each, 16 mm, Color, Sound, 1965. Rental $55.00 for 4 reels or $17.50 for each reel. Available from Appleton-Century-Crofts Film Library,

267 West 25th Street, New York, N. Y. 10001. Also available from Psychological Cinema Register, Audio-Visual Services, The Pennsylvania State University, University Park, Pennsylvania 16802, rental $30.00 for 4 reels, or $7.50 for each reel; and from Bureau of Audiovisual Education, The University of North Carolina, 111 Abernathy Hall, Chapel Hill, North Carolina 27514. $28.00 for 4 reels, or $7.00 for each reel.

Explains and demonstrates various principles and laboratory procedures of behavior modification including schedules of reinforcement, shaping, generalization, discrimination, extinction, punishment, avoidance conditioning, etc. Because of their technical level and emphasis on basic research demonstrations, these films would be more suitable for courses in general and educational psychology, learning, teacher training, etc.

236. Skinner, B. F. *A demonstration of behavioral processes.* 28 minutes, 16 mm, Color, Sound, 1971. Rental $30.00. Available from Appleton-Century-Crofts Film Library, 267 West 25th St., New York, New York 10001.

Professor Skinner explains basic operant conditioning principles to a class of university students and shows how reinforcement is the basis for behavior modification and determines the development, maintenance, and extinction of particular behaviors. Although pigeons are used to demonstrate the essentials of behavior modification, relevant extensions and applications to human behavior are discussed.

237. Skinner, B. F. *Learning and behavior: What makes us human.* CBS Conquest Film, narrated by Charles Collingwood, 26 minutes, 16 mm, Black and White, 1960. Rental $7.00. Available from Bureau of Audiovisual Education, The University of North Carolina, 111 Abernathy Hall, Chapel Hill, North Carolina 27514. Also available from Extension Media Center, University of California, Berkeley, California 94720, rental $11.00.

Professor Skinner demonstrates several basic operant reinforcement principles and procedures with the pigeon including shaping behavior, generalization, intermittent reinforcement, schedules of reinforcement, etc., and discusses the application of these same procedures with humans with particular reference to the teaching machine, programmed instruction, and facilitating learning in children.

238. Ulrich, R. *Understanding aggression.* 29 minutes, 16 mm, Color, Sound, 1972. Rental $45.00. Available from Appleton-Century-Crofts Film Library, 267 West 25th St., New York, New York 10001.

Concerned with behavioral and other variables that are functionally related to aggression including pain, punishment, aversive environmental conditions, glorification of violence, etc. Points up the necessity of moving away from dependence on aversive environments to control human beings as well as the importance of reducing the reinforcing value of aggressive behaviors in human interactions.

239. Ulrich, R. *Cure to prevention.* 30 minutes, 16 mm, Black and White, Sound, 1968. Rental $25.00. Available from Behavior Research and Development Center, Western Michigan University, Kalamazoo, Michigan 49001.

Shows the application of operant reinforcement procedures to infant and preschool children in accelerating positive and decelerating unproductive behaviors. Includes such examples as a six-month-old infant learning to imitate sounds with food as the reinforcer, a four-year-old girl teaching a two-and-one-half-year-old girl to read, and a five-year-old boy reading portions of a college textbook.

240. Wolf, M. and Phillips, E. *Achievement Place.* 30 minutes, 16 mm, Black and White, Sound, 1970. Rental $5.00 (day); $8.00 (week). Available from the University of Kansas, Bureau of Visual Instruction, 6 Bailey Hall, Lawrence, Kansas 66044. Also available from Psychological Cinema Register, Audio Visual Services, The Pennsylvania State University, University Park, Pennsylvania 16802, rental $7.70.

Shows an applied research demonstration project involving a foster home for six to eight predelinquent and delinquent boys designed to increase academic and social and decrease antisocial behaviors. Behavior modification procedures including a token reinforcement system were continuously carried out by the foster parents in this successful, innovative intervention project. For reports and material on Achievement Place, see 168 and 181.

241. Wright, J. J. *Very good, Bobby.* 35 minutes, 16 mm, Black and White, Sound, 1970. No rental fee. Available from Dr. John J. Wright, Florida Division of Mental Health, 425 Larson Building, 200 East Gaines St., Tallahassee, Florida 32304.

This film was produced to train mothers of preschool children from low income families to use operant reinforcement procedures to facilitate and accelerate language development. It shows a graded series of examples with children, one through three years of age, illustrating a variety of speech sounds and combinations. Would be helpful as a training aid for work with mothers and teachers of preschool-age children.

Author Index

Subject Index

103

School Psychology, Counseling, Social Work, etc., 57, 71, 74, 88, 94, 113, 114, 116, 119, 146.
Self-control of Reinforcements, 24, 102, 106, 110, 167, 173, 191, 193, 229.
Self-injurious Behaviors, 1, 11, 29, 43, 167, 179, 186.
Sex Problems, 25, 88, 129, 173.
Sibling Conflicts, 20, 24, 25, 26, 129, 136, 142.
Sleeping Problems, 7, 25, 37, 44, 129, 171.
Special Education Classes, 15, 50, 51, 55, 56, 66, 68, 71, 81, 91, 101, 142, 143, 157.
Speech (See Language and Speech Problems).
Teacher Aides, Volunteers, Behavior Technicians, etc., 80, 102, 106, 112, 125, 135, 140, 141, 142, 163, 167, 185, 212, 220.
Teachers—Training in Behavior Modification; Child Management Training Programs for Teachers—General, 48, 49, 50, 52-56, 58, 61, 62, 63, 70-73, 75, 76, 78, 80, 81, 84, 86, 88, 90, 91, 93, 95, 98, 100, 102, 104-111, 113, 115, 117, 121, 122, 125, 126, 133, 135, 142, 143, 148, 151, 153, 159, 160, 165, 185, 212, 213, 215, 220, 230-232.
Teachers—Training in Behavior Modification; Individual Cases and Classroom Examples of Child Management by Teachers, 49, 50, 53, 54, 55, 59, 60, 62, 63, 64, 66, 67, 75-81, 83, 86-89, 92, 93, 94, 97, 98, 99, 102-107, 109, 114, 115, 123, 124, 137, 142-145, 148, 160, 167, 170, 182, 185, 186, 212, 213, 215, 219, 220, 230, 231, 232.
Teenagers, 8, 24, 25, 38, 51, 71, 80, 96, 119, 134, 136, 144, 165, 167, 168, 172, 173, 182, 188, 197, 199, 214, 215, 233.
Television Video Tapes in Training, 4, 74, 125, 200, 208.
Toilet Training, Problems, 2, 24, 25, 36, 88, 129, 143, 149, 167, 171, 186, 225.
Tokens, Point Systems, etc., 3, 8, 18, 23-26, 32-33, 42, 48, 51, 53, 54, 55, 58, 59, 62, 63, 65, 68, 69, 71, 75, 77, 79, 80, 86, 88, 91, 97, 98, 102, 103, 105-108, 111, 112, 115-118, 122, 127, 129, 130, 132, 134, 135, 136, 143, 148, 165, 167, 168, 170, 171, 173, 180, 181, 182, 184, 185, 186, 191, 221, 224, 231, 233.

105

Other Books from Research Press:

A Glossary of Behavioral Terminology
Owen R. White

How to Use Contingency Contracting in the Classroom
Lloyd Homme, et al.

Families:
Applications of Social Learning to Family Life
Gerald R. Patterson

Marriage Happiness:
A Behavioral Approach to Counseling
David Knox

New Books from Research Press:

Slim Chance in a Fat World:
Behavioral Control of Obesity. Condensed Edition.
Richard B. Stuart and Barbara Davis

After the Turn On, What?
Learning Perspectives on Humanistic Groups
Peter S. Houts and Michael Serber, Eds.

Toward a Technology for Humanizing Education
David N. Aspy